Office of Commissioner of Education Rhode Island

The School Manual

Containing the School Laws of Rhode Island

Office of Commissioner of Education Rhode Island

The School Manual
Containing the School Laws of Rhode Island

ISBN/EAN: 9783744666978

Printed in Europe, USA, Canada, Australia, Japan

Cover: Foto ©Suzi / pixelio.de

More available books at **www.hansebooks.com**

THE
SCHOOL MANUAL,

CONTAINING THE

SCHOOL LAWS OF RHODE ISLAND;

WITH

DECISIONS, REMARKS AND FORMS,

FOR THE USE OF SCHOOL OFFICERS.

1882.

Prepared in accordance with a Resolution of the General Assembly by
THOMAS B. STOCKWELL, Commissioner of Public Schools.

PROVIDENCE:
E. L. FREEMAN & CO., PRINTERS TO THE STATE.
1882.

NOTE.

This book is public property and is for the use of School Officers. It is to be delivered by each officer to his successor in office, and a copy should be accessible for consultation at all school meetings.

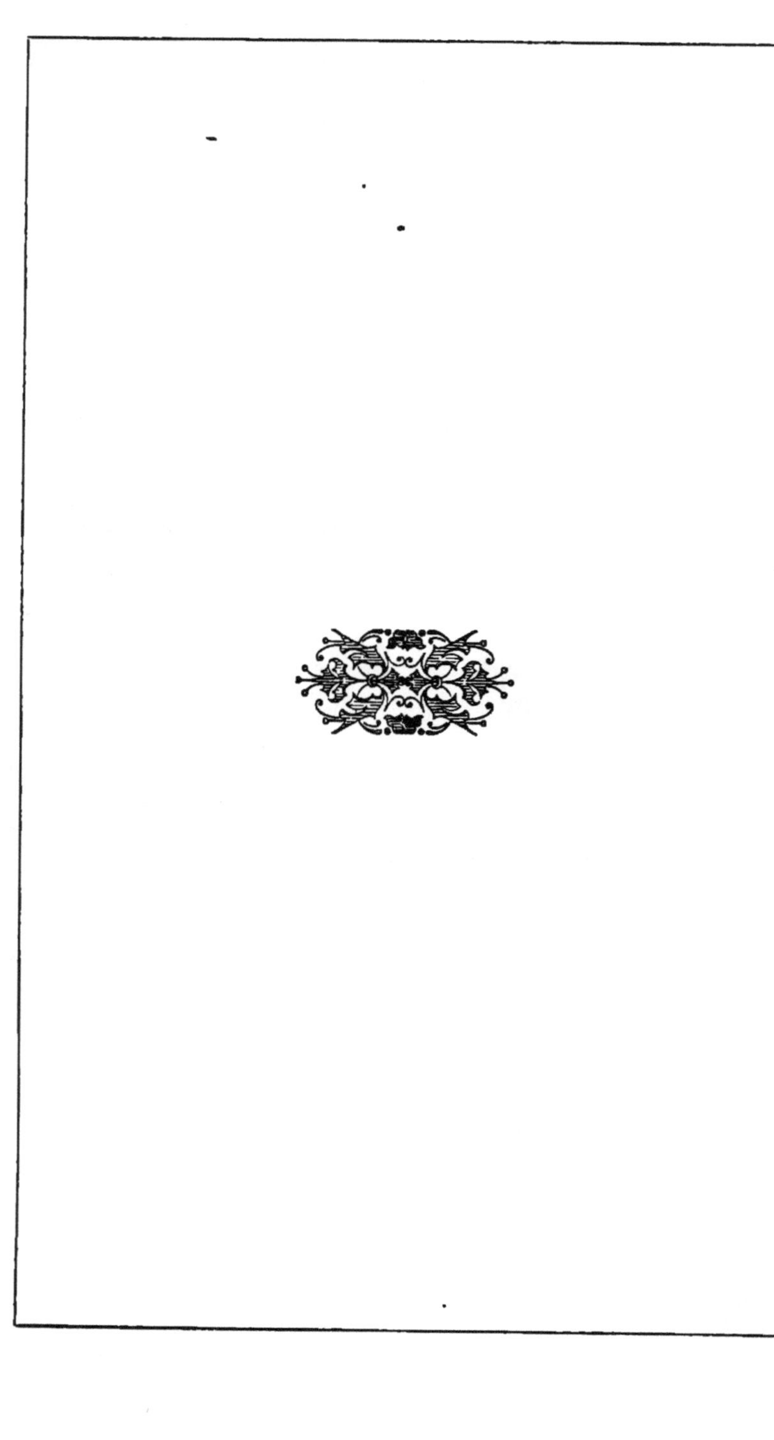

RESOLUTION

INSTRUCTING THE COMMISSIONER OF PUBLIC SCHOOLS TO PREPARE A

SCHOOL MANUAL.

(Passed January Session, 1881.)

Resolved, That the commissioner of public schools be and is hereby directed to prepare a school manual for the use of the officers of the public schools of the State, which shall contain "Title IX," of the "Public Statutes," and such decisions of the Supreme Court and the commissioners of public schools, under the school laws, and such other matter as may be deemed advisable; and to cause not exceeding two thousand copies thereof, when approved by the state board of education, to be published in the style and size of the Rhode Island Manual; and the state auditor is hereby directed to draw his order on the general treasurer for the cost of the same not to exceed seven hundred dollars, when approved by the governor.

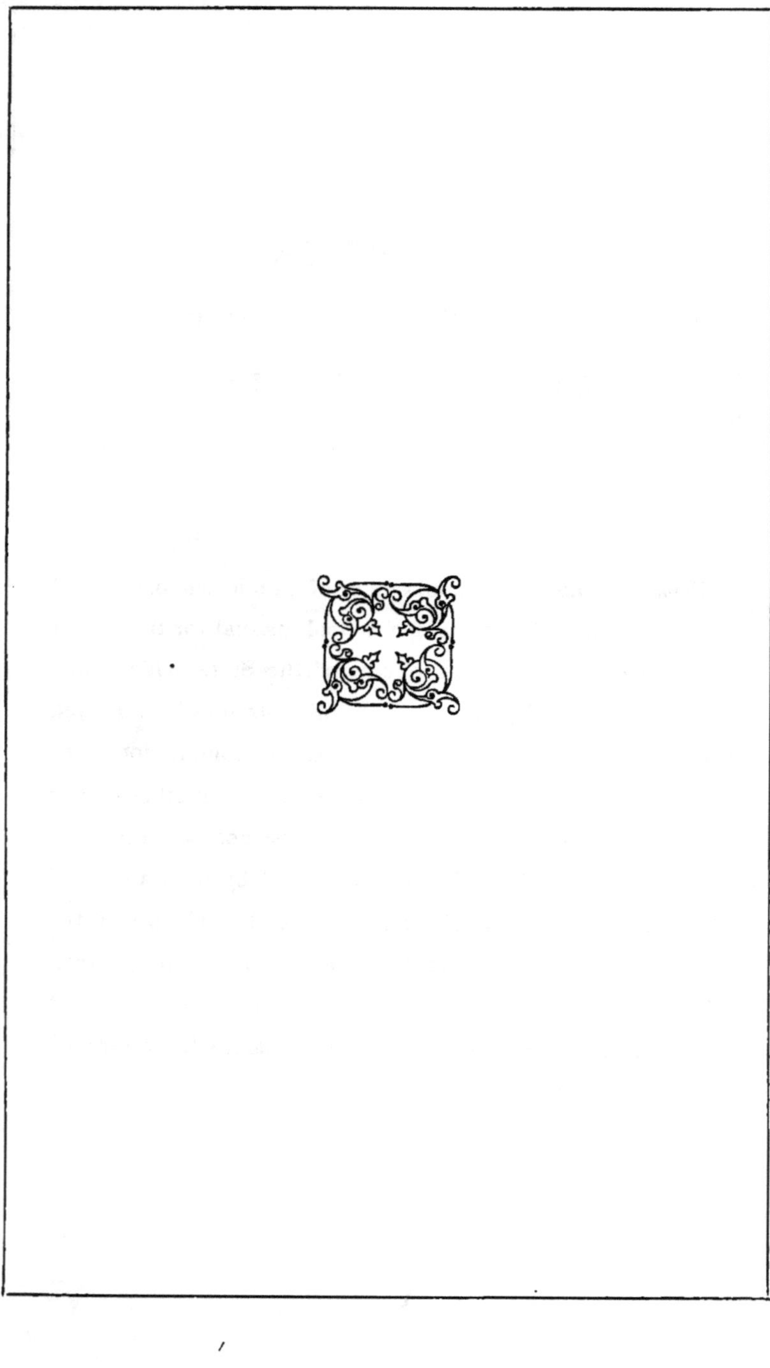

RESOLUTION OF APPROVAL

BY THE

STATE BOARD OF EDUCATION,

JUNE 8, 1882.

Resolved, That the state board of education, having examined the "School Manual" prepared by the commissioner of public schools, in accordance with the resolution passed at the January Session, 1881, hereby approve the same and order its publication.

ALFRED H. LITTLEFIELD, HENRY H. FAY, GEORGE L. LOCKE, CHARLES J. WHITE, DANIEL LEACH, DWIGHT R. ADAMS, DAVID S. BAKER, JR., LUCIUS D. DAVIS,	State Board of Education.

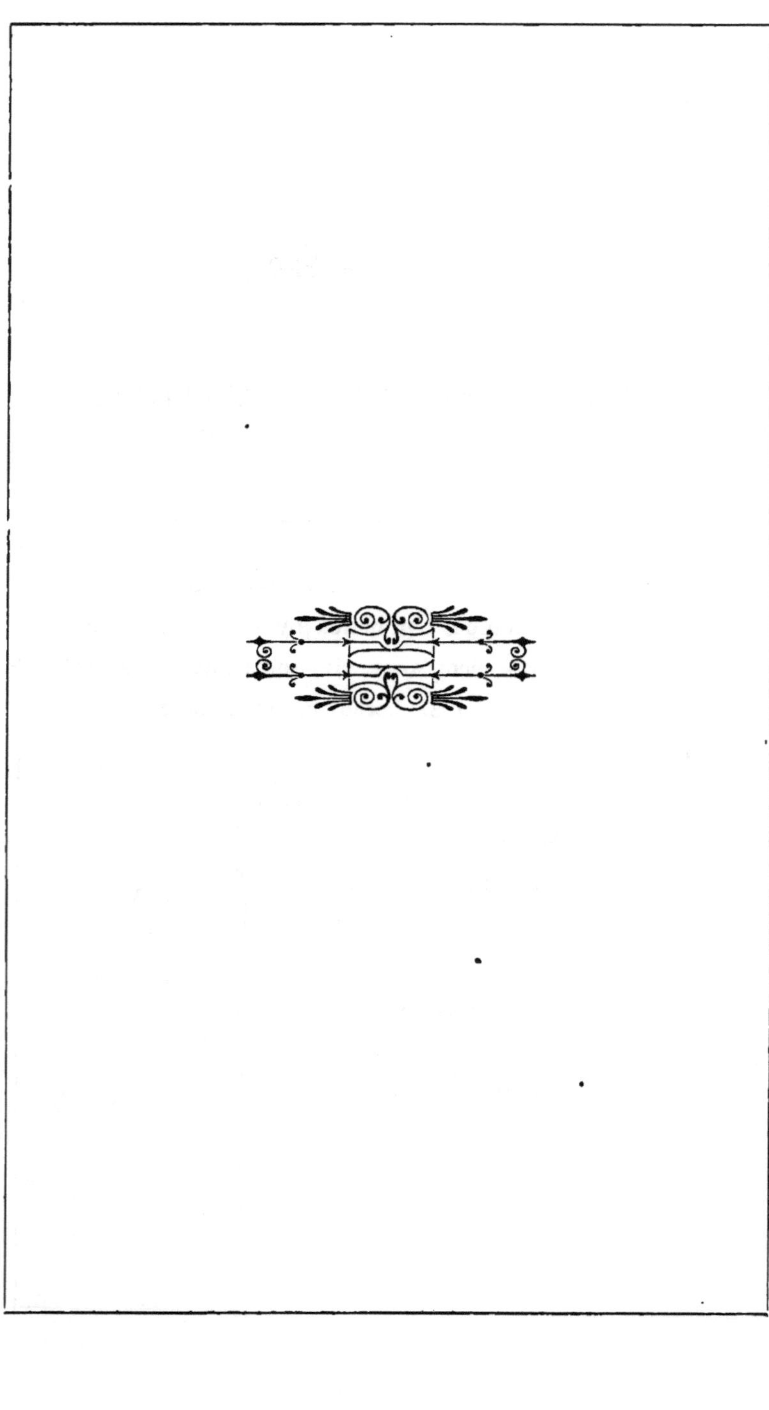

CONTENTS.

EXTRACTS FROM THE CONSTITUTION OF THE STATE.

Title XXX.

EXTRACTS FROM THE PUBLIC LAWS.

DECISIONS.

REMARKS.

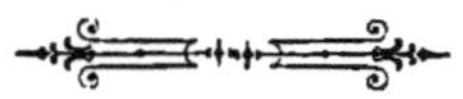

EXTRACTS

FROM THE

CONSTITUTION OF RHODE ISLAND.

PREAMBLE.

WE, the people of the State of Rhode Island and Providence Plantations, grateful to Almighty God for the civil and religious liberty which he hath so long permitted us to enjoy, and looking to Him for a blessing upon our endeavors to secure and to transmit the same unimpaired to succeeding generations, do ordain and establish this constitution of government.

ARTICLE I.

Declaration of Certain Constitutional Rights and Principles.

In order effectually to secure the religious and political freedom established by our venerated ancestors, and to preserve the same for our posterity, we do declare that the essential and unquestionable rights and principles hereinafter mentioned shall be established, maintained and preserved, and shall be of paramount obligation in all legislative, judicial and executive proceedings.

SECTION 2. All free governments are instituted for the protection, safety and happiness of the people. All laws, therefore, should be made for the good of the whole; and the burdens of the State ought to be fairly distributed among its citizens.

SEC. 3. Whereas Almighty God hath created the mind free; and all attempts to influence it by temporal punishments or burdens, or by civil incapacitations, tend to beget habits of hypocrisy and meanness; and whereas a principal object of our venerable ancestors, in their migration to this country and their settlement of this State, was, as they expressed it, to hold forth a lively experiment, that a flourishing civil State may stand and be best maintained with full liberty in religious concernments: we, therefore, declare that no man shall be compelled to frequent or to support any religious worship, place, or ministry whatever, except in fulfilment of his own voluntary contract; nor enforced, restrained, molested, or burdened in his body or goods; nor disqualified from holding any office; nor otherwise suffer on account of his religious belief; and that every man shall be free to worship God according to the dictates of his own conscience, and to profess and by argument to maintain his opinion in matters of religion; and that the same shall in no wise diminish, enlarge, or affect his civil capacity.

ARTICLE IX.

Of Qualifications for Office.

SECTION 1. No person shall be eligible to any civil office, (except the office of school committee), unless he be a qualified elector for such office.

ARTICLE XII.

Of Education.

SECTION 1. The diffusion of knowledge, as well as of virtue, among the people, being essential to the preservation of their rights and liberties, it shall be the duty of the general assembly to promote public schools, and to adopt all means which they may deem necessary and proper to secure to the people the advantages and opportunities of education.

SEC. 2. The money which now is or which may hereafter be appropriated by law for the establishment of a permanent fund for the support of public schools, shall be securely invested, and remain a perpetual fund for that purpose.

SEC. 3. All donations for the support of public

schools, or for other purposes of education, which may be received by the general assembly, shall be applied according to the terms prescribed by the donors.

Sec. 4. The general assembly shall make all necessary provisions by law for carrying this article into effect. They shall not divert said money or fund from the aforesaid uses, nor borrow, appropriate, or use the same, or any part thereof, for any other purpose, under any pretence whatsoever.

EXTRACTS FROM THE PUBLIC STATUTES

OF THE

STATE OF RHODE ISLAND

RELATING TO

PUBLIC INSTRUCTION.

IN THE YEAR OF OUR LORD 1882.

TITLE V.

CHAPTER 28.

Of the Permanent School Fund.

SECTION 1. The general treasurer, with the advice of the governor, shall have full power to regulate the custody and safe keeping of the fund now constituting the permanent fund for the support of public schools, and shall keep the same securely invested in the capital stock of some safe and responsible bank or banks or in bonds of towns or cities within this State.

Sec. 2. The money that shall be paid into the State treasury by auctioneers, for duties accruing to the use of the State, is appropriated, and the same shall annually be added to said school fund, for the permanent increase thereof.

Sec. 3. Whenever any money appropriated to any town from the State treasury, for the support of public schools therein, shall have been forfeited by such town, the same shall be added to said school fund, and shall forever remain a part thereof.

Sec. 4. The general treasurer, with the advice of the governor, shall from time to time securely invest all sums of money hereby directed to be added to said fund, in the capital stock of some safe and responsible bank or banks or in bonds of any town or city within this State.

Sec. 5. The income arising from said fund so invested shall annually be appropriated for the support of public schools in the several towns.

TITLE VII.

CHAPTER 34.

Of the Powers of, and of Suits by and against Towns.

SECTION 5. Towns may, at any legal meeting, grant and vote such sums of money as they shall judge necessary : * * * * * * * *
For the support of schools, purchase of sites for and the building and repair of school-houses ; and for the establishing and maintaining of school libraries ;
* * * * * * * * * *

SEC. 6. The electors of the city of Providence, at the annual election for members of the city council, may, by a majority vote of such electors voting, and the electors in every other town qualified to vote upon any proposition to impose a tax, or for the expenditure of money in such town, may, by a majority vote of such electors voting at the annual meeting for the election of town officers, or members of the city council therein, appropriate a sum not exceeding twenty-five cents on each one hundred dollars of the ratable property of such town in the year next preceding such appropriation, for the foundation therein of a free public library, with or without branches, for all the inhabitants thereof, and to provide suitable rooms for such library, which shall be used under such regulations as may from time to time be prescribed by the town council of such town, or city council of such city.

SEC. 7. Any town having established a free public library therein, in manner as aforesaid, may annually, by the majority vote of the electors thereof, qualified as aforesaid, and voting on the proposition, appropriate a sum not exceeding twenty cents on each one thousand dollars of its ratable property, in the year next preceding such appropriation, for the maintenance and increase of such library therein, and may take, receive, hold and manage any devise, bequest or donation for the establishment, increase or maintenance of a public library therein, to be under such regulations for its government, when they are not prescribed by its donor, as may from time to time be prescribed by the town council of such town, or the city council of such city: *Provided*, that the town of Pawtucket may appropriate a sum not exceeding thirty cents on each one thousand dollars of its ratable property.

TITLE VIII.

CHAPTER 46.

General Provisions concerning Taxes.

SECTION
1. Towns may provide for deduction, if tax is paid, and impose a percentage, if tax is not paid.
2. Officers neglecting to perform duties required of them, liable to be indicted.

SECTION
3. Town taxes to have preference, in cases of insolvency.
4. Compensation of assessors, town clerks and collectors.
5. Provisions of this title applicable to highway and school district taxes.

SECTION 1. Any town may provide for such deduction from the tax assessed against any person, if paid by an appointed time, or for such penalties by way of percentage on a tax, if not paid at the time appointed, not exceeding twelve per centum per annum, as they shall deem necessary to insure punctual payment.

SEC. 2. Every officer who shall neglect or refuse to perform any duty imposed on him in this title, or who shall not comply with the provisions thereof, or who shall in anywise knowingly violate any provisions thereof, shall be imprisoned not exceeding one year or be fined not exceeding five hundred dollars, which fine, in case it be a state tax, shall be paid into the state treasury, or if a town tax, into the town treasury, or if a school district tax, into the school district treasury, or if a fire corporation tax, into the fire corporation treasury.

SEC. 3. Whenever any person shall become insolvent, or die insolvent, town taxes due from him or his estate shall have preference, after debts or taxes due the United States and this state, over all other debts or demands, save those due for necessary funeral charges, and for attendance and medicine during his last sickness.

SEC. 4. Assessors shall receive such compensation as the town shall allow; town clerks shall be paid for copying tax bills as for other copies; and collectors shall be paid for collecting at the rate of five per centum, unless they shall have agreed with the town for a less sum; which fees shall be paid out of the town treasury. In case of distraint of personal property, or levy on land, the collector shall have the same fees as sheriffs have in similar cases.

SEC. 5. The provisions of this title shall apply to all highway and school district taxes, so far as they may be applicable.

TITLE IX.

OF PUBLIC INSTRUCTION.

CHAPTER 47.

Of the Board of Education.

SECTION 1. The general supervision and control of the public schools of the state, with such high schools, normal schools and normal institutes, as are or may be established and maintained wholly or in part by the state, shall be vested in a state board of education, which shall consist of the governor and the lieutenant-governor as members, by virtue of their office, and of one other member from each of the counties of the state, with the exception of Providence county, which shall have two other members. The board of education shall elect the commissioner of public schools.

SEC. 2. The members of the board of education shall continue to be divided into three classes, and to hold their offices until the terms for which they were respectively elected shall have expired.

SEC. 3. Two members of the board of education shall be elected annually at the May session of the general assembly, in grand committee, from the counties in which vacancies shall occur in said board, who shall hold office for three years, and until their successors shall have been elected and qualified; vacancies in said board shall be filled for any unexpired term by an election from the county for which the member whose office is vacant was elected, in the same manner, at any session of the general assembly.

SEC. 4. The governor shall be president, and the commissioner of public schools shall be secretary of the board of education.

SEC. 5. The board of education shall hold quarterly meetings in the first week of March, June, September and December of each year, at the office of the commissioner of public schools, and may hold special meetings at the call of the president or secretary. They shall prescribe, and cause to be enforced, all rules and regulations necessary for carrying into effect the laws in relation to public schools.

SEC. 6. The board of education may cause to be paid annually to and for the use of each free public library established and maintained in the state, and to be expended in the purchase of books therefor, a sum not exceeding fifty dollars for the first five hundred volumes included in such library, and twenty-five dollars for every additional five hundred volumes therein: *Provided*, that the annual payment for the benefit of any one such library shall not exceed the sum of five hundred dollars.

SEC. 7. The board of education shall from time to time establish rules prescribing the character of the books which shall constitute such a library as will be entitled to the benefits conferred by the preceding section, regulating the management of such library so as to secure the free use of the same to the people of the town and neighborhood in which it shall be established, and directing the mode in which the sums paid in pursuance of this chapter shall be expended. No library shall receive any benefit under the foregoing provisions, unless such rules shall have been complied with by those in charge thereof, nor until they shall have furnished to said board satisfactory evidence of the number and character of the books contained in said library.

SEC. 8. Every payment herein authorized shall be made by the general treasurer upon the order of the commissioner of public schools, approved by the board

2

of education, and payable to the librarian or other person having charge of such library or of the funds applied to its support designated by said board.

SEC. 9. The board of education shall make an annual report to the general assembly at the adjourned session in Providence.

SEC. 10. The members of said board shall receive no compensation for their services, but the general treasurer shall pay, upon the order of the state auditor, the necessary expenses of the members, when attending the meetings of the board, or when travelling on official business within the state, after the bills have been approved by the general assembly.

CHAPTER 48.

Of the Commissioner of Public Schools.

SECTION 1. There shall be annually elected a commissioner of public schools in the manner prescribed in the preceding chapter, who shall devote his time exclusively to the duties of his office. In case of sickness, temporary absence, or other disability, the governor may appoint a person to act as commissioner during such absence, sickness or disability.

SEC. 2. He may employ a clerk to assist in the duties of his office at an annual compensation not exceeding five hundred dollars.

SEC. 3. The commissioner of public schools shall visit, as often as practicable, every school district in the state, for the purpose of inspecting the schools, and diffusing as widely as possible, by public addresses and personal communications with school officers, teachers and parents, a knowledge of the defects, and of any desirable improvements in the administration of the system and the government and instruction of the schools.

SEC. 4. He shall, under the direction of the board of education, recommend and bring about, as far as practicable, a uniformity of text-books in the schools of all the towns; and shall assist in the establishment of, and selection of books for, school libraries.

SEC. 5. He shall annually, in December, make a report to the board of education, upon the state and condition of the schools and of education, with plans and suggestions for the improvement of said schools.

CHAPTER 49.

Of the Appropriations for Public Schools.

SECTION 1. The sum of ninety thousand dollars shall be annually paid out of the income of the permanent school fund, and from other money in the treasury, for the support of public schools in the several towns, on the order of the commissioner of public schools.

SEC. 2. The sum of sixty-three thousand dollars of the amount aforesaid shall be apportioned annually, in May, by the commissioner of public schools among the several towns, in proportion to the number of children therein under the age of fifteen years, according to the census of the United States, or of this state, then last preceding; and the sum of twenty-seven thousand dollars shall be apportioned among the several towns in proportion to the number of school districts in each town.

SEC. 3. The money appropriated from the state as aforesaid shall be denominated teachers' money, and shall be applied to the wages of teachers, and to no other purpose.

SEC. 4. No town shall receive any part of such state appropriation, unless it shall raise by tax for the support of public schools, a sum equal to the amount it may receive from the treasury for the support of public schools.

SEC. 5. If any town shall neglect or refuse to raise or appropriate the sum required in the preceding section on or before the first day of July, in any year, its proportion of the public money shall be forfeited, and the general treasurer, on being informed thereof in writing by the commissioner of public schools, shall add it to the permanent school fund.

SEC. 6. The commissioner of public schools shall

draw orders on the general treasurer for their proportion of the appropriation for public schools, in favor of all such towns as shall on or before the first day of July annually comply with the conditions of section four of this chapter.

SEC. 7. The sum of three thousand dollars shall be annually appropriated for the purchase of dictionaries, encyclopedias and other works of reference, maps, globes and other apparatus for the use of the public schools of the state.

SEC. 8. Said sum of three thousand dollars shall be apportioned among the several towns and districts as follows: Every town or district desiring to avail itself of this appropriation shall make application therefor to the commissioner of public schools, and with said application shall file proper vouchers that at least an amount equal to that asked for from the state has been raised or appropriated for the same purpose by the town or district. Upon the receipt of said application and vouchers, the commissioner of public schools may draw his order on the general treasurer in favor of said applicant to an amount not to exceed fifty dollars in any one year, in favor of any town not divided into districts, and not to exceed twenty dollars in favor of any district: *Provided*, that the gross amount in any one fiscal year shall not exceed three thousand dollars.

SEC. 9. In case the number and amount of applications in any one fiscal year shall exceed the limit of the appropriation, the commissioner of public schools shall record the date of each application, and in the apportionment for the following year such recorded applications shall have the preference in the order of their dates.

Sec. 10. There shall be an annual appropriation for the support and maintenance of evening schools in the several towns of this state, under the general supervision of the state board of education, who shall apportion said appropriation annually among the several towns, and draw orders therefor on the general treasurer.

CHAPTER 50.

Of the Powers and Duties of Towns and of the Town Treasurer and Town Clerk relative to Public Schools.

Section 1. Every town shall establish and maintain, with or without forming districts, a sufficient number of public schools, at convenient places, under the management of the school committee, subject to the supervision of the commissioner of public schools as provided by this title.

SEC. 2. Any town may be divided by a vote thereof, into school districts.

SEC. 3. Any town may vote, in a meeting notified for that purpose, to provide school-houses, together with the necessary fixtures and appendages thereof, in all the districts, if there be districts, at the common expense of the town: *Provided*, that if any district shall provide, at its own expense, a school-house approved by the school committee, such district shall not be liable to be taxed by the town to provide or repair school-houses for the other districts.

SEC. 4. The school committee of each town shall consist of three residents of the town, or of such number as at the present time constitute the committee, and they shall be divided as equally as may be, into three classes, whose several terms of office shall expire at the end of three years from the dates of their respective elections; and in the case of the first election of a school committee under this chapter, the terms of office of the three classes shall be respectively one year, two years and three years; the classes and their terms of office to be determined by lot by the committee at their first meeting after their election. As the office of each class shall become vacant, such vacancy or vacancies shall be filled by the town at its annual town meeting for the election of state or town officers, or by the town council at its next meeting thereafter. In case of a vacancy by death, resignation, or otherwise than is above provided, such vacancy shall be filled by the town council, until the next annual town meeting for state or town officers, when it shall be filled for the unexpired term thereof as is above provided.

Sec. 5. Any town at its annual town meeting may elect, or failing to do so, its school committee shall appoint, a superintendent of the schools of the town, to perform, under the advice and direction of the committee, such duties, and to exercise such powers as the committee shall assign to him, and to receive such compensation out of the town treasury as the town shall vote. In case of a vacancy it shall be filled until the next annual town meeting by the school committee.

Sec. 6. The town treasurer shall receive the money due the town from the state for public schools, and shall keep a separate account of all money appropriated by the state or town or otherwise for public schools in the town, and shall pay the same to the order of the school committee, and he shall credit the public school account, on the first Monday of May in each year, with the total amount of money received by him for registry taxes during the year ending the thirtieth day of April last preceding.

Sec. 7. The town treasurer shall, before the first day of July in each year, submit to the school committee a statement of all moneys applicable to the support of public schools for the current school year specifying the sources of the same.

Sec. 8. The town treasurer shall, on or before the first day of July, annually, transmit to the commissioner of public schools a certificate of the amount which the town has voted to raise by tax for the support of public schools for the current year; and also a statement of the amount paid out to the order of the school committee and from what sources it was derived for the year ending the thirtieth day of April next preceding; and until such return is made to the commissioner, he may, in his discretion, withhold the order for the money in the state treasury belonging to such town.

SEC. 9. The town clerk shall record the boundaries of school districts and all alterations thereof in a book to be kept for that purpose, and shall distribute such school documents and blanks as shall be sent to him to the persons for whom they are intended.

SEC. 10. The town clerks, or some person whom the board of aldermen of any city, or the town council of any town shall appoint for the purpose, shall annually, in the month of January, take or cause to be taken, a census of all persons between the ages of five and fifteen years inclusive, residing within the limits of their respective towns on the first day of said January.

SEC. 11. The blank forms required to carry out the requirements of the preceding section shall be furnished by the commissioner of public schools to each town, on or before the first day of December in each year, and they shall call in substance for the following information, namely, the name, age, number of weeks' attendance upon any school, parents' name and residence, of each person enumerated.

SEC. 12. The returns of said census shall be alphabetically arranged and deposited in the hands of the school committees of the several towns on or before the first day of April in each year; and the receipt of the chairman or clerk of the school committee to the effect that the above returns have been so received by him shall be forwarded to the commissioner of public schools, before he shall draw his order for the payment of any portion of the public money to that town.

CHAPTER 51.

Of the Powers of School Districts and School Officers.

SECTION 1. Every school district shall be a body corporate, and shall be known by its number, or other suitable designation.

SEC. 2. Every school district may prosecute and defend in all actions in which said district or its officers are parties, may purchase, receive, hold and convey real or personal property for school purposes, and may establish and maintain a school library.

SEC. 3. Every such district may build, purchase, hire and repair school-houses, and supply the same with blackboards, maps, furniture and other necessary and useful appendages, and may insure the house and appendages against damage by fire: *Provided*, that the erection and repairs of the school-house shall be made according to the plans approved by the school committee, or on appeal, by the commissioner of public schools.

Sec. 4. Every such district may raise money by tax on the ratable property of the district, to support public schools, and to carry out the powers given them by any of the provisions of this title: *Provided*, that the amount of the tax shall be approved by the school committee of the town.

Sec. 5. Every such district shall annually elect a moderator, a clerk, a treasurer, a collector and either one or three trustees, as the district shall decide, and may fill vacancies in either of said offices at any legal meeting. The moderator may administer the oath of office to all the other officers of the school district.

Sec. 6. The clerk, collector and treasurer, within their respective school districts, shall have the like power, and shall perform like duties, as the clerk, collector and treasurer of a town; but the clerk, collector and treasurer need not give bond, unless required by the district.

Sec. 7. All district taxes shall be collected by the district or town collector, in the same manner as town taxes are collected.

Sec. 8. Any district may vote to place the collection of any district tax in the hands of the collector of town taxes, who shall thereupon be fully authorized to proceed and collect the same, upon giving bond therefor to the district, satisfactory to the school committee.

SEC. 9. If any school district shall neglect to organize, or if organized, shall for any space of six months, neglect to establish a school and employ a teacher, the school committee of the town may themselves or by an agent establish a school in the district school-house, or elsewhere in the district, in their discretion, and employ a teacher.

SEC. 10. Any district may, with the consent of the school committee, devolve all the powers and duties relating to public schools in the district on the school committee.

CHAPTER 52.

Of District Meetings.

SECTION 1. Notice of the time, place and object of holding the first meeting of a district for organization, or for a meeting to choose officers or transact other business, in case there be no trustees authorized to call a meeting, shall be given by the school committee of the town at such time and in such manner as they may deem proper.

SEC. 2. Every school district when organized shall hold an annual meeting in the month of April of each year, for choice of officers and for the transaction of any other business relating to schools.

SEC. 3. The trustees may call a special meeting for election or other business at any time, and shall call one to be held within seven days on the written request of any five qualified electors stating the object for which they wish it called; and if the trustees neglect or refuse to call a special meeting when requested, the school committee may call it and fix the time therefor.

SEC. 4. District meetings shall be held in the school-house, unless otherwise ordered by the district. If there be no school-house, or place appointed by the district for district meetings, the trustees, or if there be no trustees, the school committee shall determine the place, which shall always be within the district.

SEC. 5. Notice of the time and place of every annual meeting, and of the time, place and object of every special meeting shall be given, either by publishing the same in a newspaper published in the district, or by posting the same in two or more public places in the district for five days before holding the same.

SEC. 6. Every person residing in the district may vote in district meetings, to the same extent and with the same restrictions as he might at the time vote in town meeting; but no person shall vote upon any question of taxation of property, or expending money raised thereby, unless he shall have paid or be liable to pay, a portion of the tax.

SEC. 7. The clerk of the district shall record the number and names of the persons voting, and on which side of the question, at the request of any qualified voter.

CHAPTER 53.

Of Joint School Districts.

SECTION 1. Any two or more adjoining school districts in the same or adjoining towns, may, by a concurrent vote, establish a school for the older and more advanced children of such districts.

SEC. 2. Such associating districts shall constitute a school district for the purposes of providing a school-house, fuel, furniture and apparatus, and for the election of a board of trustees, to consist of one member from each district so associating, and for levying a tax for school purposes, with all the rights and privileges of a school district, so far as such school is concerned.

SEC. 3. The time and place for the meeting for organization of such associate district may be fixed by the school committees, and any one or more of the associating districts may delegate to the trustees of such school, the care and management of its primary school.

SEC. 4. The school committee of the town or towns in which such school shall be established, shall draw an order in favor of the trustees of such school, to be paid out of the public money appropriated to each district interested in such school, in proportion to the number of scholars from each.

SEC. 5. Any two or more adjoining school districts in the same town may, by concurrent vote, with the approbation of the school committee, unite and be consolidated into one district for the purpose of supporting public schools, and such consolidated district shall have all the powers of a single district.

SEC. 6. Such consolidated district shall be entitled to receive the same proportion of public money as such districts would receive if not united.

SEC. 7. The mode of organizing such consolidated district and calling the first meeting thereof shall be regulated or prescribed by the school committee, and notice thereof given as prescribed in section five of chapter fifty-two.

SEC. 8. Two or more adjoining districts or parts of districts, in adjoining towns, may be formed into a joint school district by the school committees of such towns concurring therein, and all joint districts which have been or shall be formed, may by them be altered or discontinued.

SEC. 9. The meeting for organization of such joint district shall be called by the school committees of such towns, and notice thereof shall be given as prescribed in section five of chapter fifty-two.

SEC. 10. Such joint district shall have all the powers of a single school district, and shall be regulated in the same manner, and shall be subject to the supervision and management of the school committee of the town in which the school is located.

SEC. 11. A whole district making a portion of such joint district, shall be entitled to its proportion of public money, in the same manner as if it had remained a single district; and whenever part of a district is taken to form a portion of such joint district, the school committee of the town of which such district is a part shall assign to it its reasonable proportion.

SEC. 12. Whenever any two or more districts shall be consolidated, the new district shall own all the corporate property of the several districts.

SEC. 13. Whenever a district is divided, and a portion taken from it, the funds and property, or the income and proceeds thereof, shall be divided among the several parts, in such manner as the school committee of the town or towns to which the districts belong, may determine.

SEC. 14. Whenever a part of one district is added to another district or part of a district owning a school-house or other property, such part shall pay to the district or part of a district to which it is added, if demanded, such sum as the school committee may determine, towards paying for such school-house and other property.

CHAPTER 54.

Of the Levy of District Taxes.

SECTION 1. District taxes shall be levied on the ratable property of the district, according to its value in the town assessment then last made, unless the district shall direct such taxes to be levied according to the next town assessment; and no notice thereof shall be required to be given by the trustees.

SEC. 2. The trustees of any school district, if unable to agree with the parties interested with regard to the valuation of any property in such district, shall call upon one or more of the town assessors not interested, and not residing in the district, to assess the value of such property so situated, in the following cases, namely: Whenever any real estate in the district is assessed in the town tax bill with real estate out of the district, so that there is no distinct or separate value upon it; whenever any person possessing personal property shall remove into the district after the last town assessment; whenever a division and apportionment of a tax shall become necessary by reason of the death of any person, or the sale of such property; whenever a person has invested personal property in real estate and shall call upon the trustees to place a value thereon; and whenever property shall have been omitted in the town valuation.

SEC. 3. The assessors shall give notice of such assessment, by posting up notices thereof for ten days next prior to such assessment, in three public places in the district; and after notice is given as aforesaid, no person neglecting to appear before the assessors shall have any remedy for being overtaxed.

SEC. 4. If a district tax shall be voted, assessed and approved of, and a contract legally entered into under it, or such contract be legally entered into without such vote, assessment or approval, and said district shall thereafter neglect or refuse to proceed to assess and collect a tax sufficient to fulfill such contract, the commissioner of public schools, after notice to and hearing of the parties, may appoint assessors to assess a tax for that purpose, and may issue a warrant to the collector of the district, or to a collector by him appointed, authorizing and requiring him to proceed and collect such tax.

SEC. 5. Errors in assessing a tax may be corrected, or the tax re-assessed, in such manner as may be directed or approved by the commissioner of public schools.

SEC. 6. Whenever any person who has paid a tax for building or repairing a school-house in one district shall, by alteration of the boundaries thereof, become liable to pay a tax in any other district, if such person cannot agree with the district, such abatement of the tax may be made as the school committee, or in case of a district composed from different towns, as the commissioner of public schools, may deem just and proper.

SEC. 7. Whenever a joint district shall vote to build or repair a school-house by tax, the amount of the tax and the plan and specifications of the building and repairs shall be approved by the school committees of the several towns, or, in case of their disagreement, by the commissioner of public schools.

SEC. 8. In case of assessing a tax by a joint or associate district, if the town assessments be made on different principles, or the relative value be not the same, the relative value and proportion shall be ascertained by one or more persons, to be appointed by the commissioner of public schools, and the assessment shall be made accordingly.

CHAPTER 55.

Of the Trustees of School Districts.

SECTION 1. The trustees of school districts shall have the custody of the school-house and other district property, and shall employ one or more qualified teachers for every fifty scholars in average daily attendance.

SEC. 2. The trustees shall provide school-rooms and fuel, and shall visit the schools twice at least during each term, and notify the committee or superintendent of the time of opening and closing the schools.

SEC. 3. The trustees shall see that the scholars are properly supplied with books, and in case they are not so supplied, and the parents, guardians or masters have been notified thereof by the teacher, shall provide the same at the expense of the district share of the town school appropriation, subject to the approval of the school committee.

SEC. 4. The trustees shall make out the tax bill against the persons liable to pay the same, and deliver the same to the collector with a warrant by them signed annexed thereto, requiring him to collect and pay over the same to the treasurer of the district.

SEC. 5. The trustees shall make returns to the school committee in manner and form prescribed by them or by the commissioner, or as may be required by law, and perform all other lawful acts required of them by the district, or necessary to carry into full effect the powers and duties of districts.

SEC. 6. The trustees shall receive no compensation for services out of the money received from either the state or town appropriations, nor in any way, unless raised by tax by the district.

SEC. 7. The trustees of any school district may allow scholars from without the town or the state, to attend the public schools of such district, on such terms as the trustees may determine: *Provided*, that such terms shall be approved by the school committee.

SEC. 8. Whenever a town shall not be divided into school districts, or whenever public schools shall be provided without reference to such division, the school committee may exercise the powers provided in the preceding section to be exercised by trustees.

SEC. 9. All moneys received for tuition as hereinbefore provided shall be paid into the district or town treasury, as the case may be, and shall be used for school purposes only.

SEC. 10. No attendance upon the public schools authorized by the preceding three sections shall be reckoned in determining the average attendance, for the purpose of regulating the distribution of school money, but such average attendance shall be returned to the district where such scholars reside, and be there reckoned with the average attendance of the schools of that district, upon demand of the trustees thereof.

CHAPTER 56.

Of the Powers and Duties of School Committees, and Apportionment and Uses of School Money.

SECTION 1. The school committee of each town shall choose a chairman and clerk, either of whom may sign any orders or official papers, and may be removed at the pleasure of said committee.

SEC. 2. The school committee shall meet at least four times in every year, and as much oftener as the state of the schools shall require. A majority of the number elected shall constitute a quorum, unless the committee consist of more than six, when four shall be a quorum, but any number may adjourn.

SEC. 3. The school committee may alter and discontinue school districts, and shall settle their boundaries when undefined or disputed; but no change shall be made in the boundaries of any district, except at a meeting, notice of which, with the proposed changes, has been posted upon the school-houses and sent to the trustees of the districts whose boundaries are liable to be affected, for at least five days before holding the same, and no new district shall be formed with less than forty children between the ages of four and sixteen, unless with the approbation of the commissioner of public schools; and the clerk of the committee shall transmit to the town clerk a certified copy of all votes affecting the boundary lines of the districts immediately on the passage thereof.

SEC. 4. The school committee shall locate all school-houses, and shall not abandon or change the location of any without good cause.

SEC. 5. In case the school committee shall fix upon a location for a school-house in any district, or shall determine that the school-house lot ought to be enlarged, and the district shall have passed a vote to erect a school-house, or to enlarge the school-house lot, or in case there is no district organization, and the committee shall fix upon a location for a school-house and the proprietor of the land shall refuse to convey the same, or cannot agree with the district for the price thereof, the school committee of their own motion, or on application of the district, may appoint three disinterested persons, who shall notify the parties and decide upon the valuation of the land; and upon the tender or payment of the sum so fixed on, to the proprietor, the title to the land so fixed on by the school committee, not exceeding one acre, shall vest in the district for the purpose of maintaining thereon a school-house and the necessary appendages thereof.

Sec. 6. An appeal in such case shall be allowed to the court of common pleas, in the same manner and with the same effect, both as to the necessity of taking the particular land condemned, and the valuation thereof, and the like proceedings thereon shall be had, as is provided by law, in case of taking land for public highways.

Sec. 7. The school committee may examine, by themselves or by some one or more persons by them appointed, every applicant for the situation of teacher in the public schools of the town, and may after five days' notice in writing annul the certificate of such as upon examination by them prove unqualified, or will not conform to the regulations of the committee, and in such case shall give immediate notice thereof to the trustee of the district in which such teacher is employed.

Sec. 8. The school committee shall visit, by one or more of their number, every public school in the town, at least twice during each term, once within two weeks of its opening, and once within two weeks of its close, at which visits they shall examine the register, and matters touching the school-house, library, studies, books, discipline, modes of teaching and improvement of the school.

Sec. 9. The school committee shall make and cause to be put up in each school-house, rules and regulations for the attendance and classification of the pupils, for the introduction and use of text-books and works of reference, and for the instruction, government and discipline of the public schools, and shall prescribe the studies to be pursued therein, under the direction of the commissioner of public schools.

SEC. 10. The school committee may suspend during pleasure all pupils found guilty of incorrigibly bad conduct or of violation of the school regulations.

SEC. 11. Where a town is not divided into districts, or shall vote in a meeting duly notified for that purpose to provide schools without reference to such division, the school committee shall manage and regulate said schools, and draw all orders for the payment of their expenses.

SEC. 12. Whenever the public schools are maintained by district organization, the committee shall apportion, among the districts, the town's proportion of the sum of sixty-three thousand dollars received from the state, one half equally, and one-half according to the average daily attendance of the schools of the preceding year.

SEC. 13. Whenever the town is divided into school districts having the management of their own concerns, the committee shall apportion equally among all the districts of the town, the town's proportion of the sum of twenty-seven thousand dollars received from the state.

SEC. 14. The school committee shall apportion the money received from the town, from the registry tax, from school funds, or from other sources, either equally or in such proportion as the town may direct, and for want of such direction, then in such manner as they deem best.

Sec. 15. The school committee shall make the apportionment among the several districts as provided in the preceding three sections on or before the first Monday of July in each year, and immediately thereafter give notice to the trustees of the amounts so apportioned to each district.

Sec. 16. The school committee shall draw an order on the town treasurer in favor of such districts only, as shall have made a return to them in manner and form prescribed by them or by the commissioner of public schools, or as may be required by law, from which it shall appear that for the year ending on the first day of May previous, one or more public schools have been kept for at least six months, by a qualified teacher, in a school-house approved by the committee or commissioner, that the money designated teachers' money, received the year previous, has been applied to the wages of teachers and to no other purpose, and that the register, properly kept, has been deposited with the committee or with some person by them appointed to receive the same.

Sec. 17. Such orders may be made payable to the trustees or their order, or to the district treasurer, or teacher, and if the treasurer receive the money, he shall pay it out to the order of the trustees.

Sec. 18. The school committee shall give no such order, until they are satisfied that the services have actually been performed for which the money is to be paid, and that the average attendance of the school has been at least five; and they shall have power, in case the average attendance of any school falls below five, to suspend said school in their discretion, and to make such other provision as they may deem best, for the attendance of the children properly belonging to said school, upon some other public school; but such suspension shall not work the forfeiture of the public money to any district, provided for by section 16 of this chapter. The school committee may allow scholars residing in one district to attend school in any other district.

SEC. 19. At the end of the school year, any money appropriated to any district which shall be forfeited, and the forfeiture not remitted, or which shall remain unexpended, shall be divided by the committee among the districts the following year.

SEC. 20. The school committee shall prepare and submit annually to the commissioner of public schools, on or before the first day of July, a report in manner and form by him prescribed, and until such report is made to the commissioner, he may refuse to draw his order for the money in the state treasury belonging to such town: *Provided*, that the necessary blank for said report has been furnished by the commissioner on or before the first day of May, next preceding; they shall also prepare and submit annually at the annual town meeting, a report to the town, setting forth their doings, the state and condition of the schools and plans for their improvement, which report, unless printed, shall be read in open town meeting. and if printed, at least three copies shall be transmitted to the commissioner on or before the first day of July in each year.

Sec. 21. The school committee may reserve annually, out of the public appropriation, a sum not exceeding forty dollars, to defray the expense of printing their annual report.

Sec. 22. A change may be made in the school-books in the public schools of any town by a vote of two-thirds of the whole school committee; and in the city of Providence by a vote of a majority of all the members elected to the school committee, notice of the proposed change having been given in writing at a previous regular meeting of said committee: *Provided*, that no change be made in any text-book in the public schools of any town oftener than once in three years, unless by the consent of the board of education.

CHAPTER 57.

Of Teachers.

Section 1. No person shall be employed by any trustee to teach as principal or assistant in any school, supported entirely or in part by the public money, unless he shall have a certificate of qualification, signed either by the school committee of the town or by some person appointed by said committee, or by the trustees of the normal school.

SEC. 2. Such certificate, unless annulled, if signed by the school committee, shall be valid within the town for one year, or for such portion thereof as shall be specified in said certificate.

SEC. 3. The school committee shall not sign any certificate of qualification unless the person named in the same shall produce evidence of good moral character, and be found on examination qualified to teach the various branches required to be taught in the school.

SEC. 4. The school committee of any town may, on reasonable notice and a hearing of such teacher, dismiss any teacher for refusal to conform to the regulations by them made, or for other just cause, and in such case shall give immediate notice to the trustees of the district.

SEC. 5. Every teacher in any public school shall keep a register of the names of all the scholars attending said school, their sex, age, names of parents or guardians, the time when each scholar enters and leaves the school, the daily attendance, together with the days of the month on which the school is visited by any officer connected with public schools, and shall prepare the return of the district to the school committee of the town.

SEC. 6. No superintendent of schools, or member of the school committee of any town, or trustee of any school district shall, so long as he continues in said office of superintendent, member of the school committee or trustee of school district, be eligible or employed to teach as principal or assistant in any school, supported entirely or in part by the public money, within the town where said superintendent, member of the school committee or trustee resides.

SEC. 7. Every teacher shall aim to implant and cultivate in the minds of all children committed to his care the principles of morality and virtue.

CHAPTER 58.

Of Legal Proceedings relating to Public Schools.

SECTION 1. Any person aggrieved by any decision or doings of any school committee, district meeting, trustees or in any other matter arising under this title, may appeal to the commissioner of public schools, who, after notice to the party interested of the time and place of hearing, shall examine and decide the same without cost to the parties: *Provided*, that nothing contained in this section shall be so construed as to deprive such aggrieved party of any legal remedy.

SEC. 2. The commissioner of public schools may, and if requested on hearing such appeal by either party shall, lay a statement of the facts of the case before one of the justices of the supreme court, whose decision shall be final.

SEC. 3. The commissioner of public schools may from time to time prescribe rules regulating the time and manner of taking such appeals, and rules to prevent appeals for trifling and frivolous causes.

SEC. 4. Parties having any matter of dispute between them arising under this title may agree in writing to submit the same to the adjudication of said commissioner, and his decision therein shall be final.

SEC. 5. If no appeal be taken from a vote of a district relating to the ordering of a tax, or from the proceedings of the officers of the district in assessing the same, or if on appeal, such proceedings are confirmed, the same shall not again be questioned before any court of law or magistrate whatsoever: *Provided*, that this section shall not be so construed as to dispense with legal notice of the meeting, or with the approval of the votes or proceedings by the school committee or commissioner of public schools, whenever the same is required by law.

SEC. 6. In any civil suit before any court, against any school officer, for any matter which might by this chapter have been heard and decided by the commissioner of public schools, no costs shall be taxed for the plaintiff, if the court are of opinion that such officer acted in good faith.

SEC. 7. Any inhabitant of a district, or person liable to pay taxes therein, may be allowed by any court to answer a suit brought therein against the district, on giving security for costs, in such manner as the court may direct.

SEC. 8. Whenever judgment shall be recovered in any court of record against any school district, the court rendering judgment shall order a warrant to be issued, if no appeal be taken, to the assessors of taxes of the town in which such district is situated, or in case of a joint district, composed of parts of towns, then to one or more of the assessors of each town, with or without designating them, requiring them to assess upon the ratable property in said district a tax sufficient to pay the debts or damages, costs, interest and a sum in the discretion of the court sufficient to defray the expenses of assessment and collection. Said assessors shall, without a new engagement, proceed to assess the same, giving notice as in case of other district taxes.

SEC. 9. Said warrant shall also contain a direction to the collector of the town, or in case of a joint district, then to the collector of either town, as the court may direct, requiring him to collect said tax; and said warrant, with the assessment annexed thereto, shall be a sufficient authority for the collector, without a special engagement, to proceed and collect the same with the same power as in case of a town tax; and when collected, he shall pay over the same to the parties to whom it may belong, and the surplus, if any, to the district. And the court may require a bond of the collector.

Sec. 10. Whenever any writ, summons or other process shall issue against any school district in any civil suit, the same may be served on the treasurer or clerk, and if there are no such officers to be found, the officer charged with the same may post up a certified copy thereof on the door of the school-house, and if there be no school-house, then in some public place in the district, and the same, when proved to the satisfaction of the court, shall constitute a sufficient service thereof.

Sec. 11. The record of the district clerk that a meeting has been duly or legally notified shall be *prima facie* evidence that it has been notified as the law requires. The clerk shall obtain at the expense of the district a suitably bound book for keeping the record therein.

Sec. 12. The commissioner of public schools may, by and with the advice and consent of the board of education, remit all fines, penalties and forfeitures incurred by any town, district or person, under any of the provisions of this title, except the forfeiture incurred by any town for not raising its proportion of money.

CHAPTER 59.

Of the Normal School, Teachers' Institutes and Lectures.

SEC. 1. The normal school shall be under the management of the board of education and the commissioner of public schools as a board of trustees.

SEC. 2. All applicants from the several towns in the state shall be admitted to free tuition in said school, after having passed such an examination as may be prescribed by the board of trustees, and after having given to such board satisfactory evidence of their intention to teach in the public schools of this state for at least one year after leaving the said school.

SEC. 3. Persons who shall have passed the regular course of studies at the normal school shall, on the written recommendation of the principal, receive a diploma signed by the trustees of the school.

SEC. 4. The said trustees may, by themselves or by a committee of their board, examine all applicants to teach in the public schools, and shall give certificates to such as are found qualified to teach school.

SEC. 5. The trustees of the normal school may pay

to each pupil who shall reside within the state, and not within five miles of said school, who shall have been duly admitted thereto, and who shall have attended the regular sessions of said school and complied with the regulations thereof, during the term next preceding such payments, not exceeding ten dollars for each quarter year, for travelling expenses, but such payments in the aggregate for such travelling expenses shall not exceed the sum of fifteen hundred dollars in any one year, and shall be made to the respective pupils entitled to the same, in proportion to the distance they may reside from said school.

SEC. 6. A sum not exceeding five hundred dollars shall be annually paid for defraying the necessary expenses and charges for teachers and lecturers for teachers' institutes, to be holden under the direction of the commissioner of public schools; and a sum not exceeding three hundred dollars shall be annually paid under the direction of the board of education for publishing and distributing among the several towns educational publications, providing lectures on educational topics and otherwise promoting the interests of education in the state.

SEC. 7. The commissioner of public schools shall render an annual account to the state auditor of his expenditures under the provisions of this chapter with his vouchers therefor.

CHAPTER 60.

Of Truant Children and Absentees from School.

SEC. 1. Town councils shall make needful provisions and arrangements concerning habitual truants, and children not attending school or without any regular and lawful occupation, or growing up in ignorance, between the ages of six and sixteen years, and also all such ordinances respecting such children as shall be deemed most conducive to their welfare and to the good order of such town, and may provide penalties for the breach of any such ordinance, not exceeding twenty dollars for any one offence.

SEC. 2. Any such minor, convicted under any such ordinance of being an habitual truant, or of not attending school, or of being without any lawful occupation, or of growing up in ignorance, may, at the discretion of the court having jurisdiction of the case, instead of being fined as aforesaid, be committed to any institution of instruction or suitable situation provided for that purpose.

SEC. 3. Any town council or board of aldermen may designate the industrial school in the city of Providence as the institution of instruction or suitable situation provided for in the preceding section.

SEC. 4. Before any ordinances made under the authority of the preceding three sections shall take effect, they shall be approved by the commissioner of public schools.

SEC. 5. The general treasurer shall pay to the managers of the industrial school of the city of Providence a sum not exceeding two dollars per week for the board, clothing and instruction of children committed to said school from any town, in accordance with the provisions of this chapter.

SEC. 6. The several towns, availing themselves of the provisions of this chapter shall appoint, at their annual town meetings, or annually, by their town councils, three or more persons, who alone shall be authorized to make the complaints in case of violation of said ordinances, and said persons thus appointed shall alone have authority to carry into execution the judgment of said court.

SEC. 7. The municipal court of the city of Providence and the justice courts of the city of Newport and of the several towns shall have jurisdiction of all cases arising under this chapter.

CHAPTER 61.

General Provisions relating to Public Schools.

SECTION 1. No person shall be excluded from any public school in the district to which such person belongs, if the town is divided into districts, or, if not so divided, from the nearest public school, on account of race or color, or for being over fifteen years of age, nor except by force of some general regulation applicable to all persons under the same circumstances.

SEC. 2. Every school district officer elected or appointed under the provisions of this title, except the moderator of a district meeting, shall take an engagement before some person authorized to administer oaths, to support the constitution of the United States, the constitution and laws of this state, and faithfully to discharge the duties of his office so long as he shall continue therein.

Sec. 3. The record of the district clerk that any school district officer has been duly engaged, shall be *prima facie* evidence thereof; and no school district officer shall enter upon the duties of his office, without taking an engagement.

Sec. 4. Every school district officer elected or appointed under the provisions of this title shall, without a new engagement, hold his office until the time of the next annual election or appointment for such office, and until his successor is elected or appointed and qualified.

Sec. 5. Every officer who shall make any false certificate, or appropriate any public school money to any purpose not authorized by law, or who shall refuse for a reasonable charge to give certified copies of any official paper, or to account for or deliver to his successor any accounts, papers or money in his hands, or shall wilfully or knowingly refuse to perform any duty of his office, or violate any provisions of any law regulating public schools, except where a particular penalty may be prescribed, shall be fined not exceeding five hundred dollars, or be imprisoned not exceeding six months, and shall be liable to an action of the case for damages, to be brought by any person injured thereby.

Sec. 6. Any school receiving aid from the state, either by direct grant or by exemption from taxation, may be visited and examined by the school committee of the town, in which such school is situated, and by the members of the board of education and the commissioner of public schools, whenever they shall deem it advisable.

Sec. 7. Whenever such school shall refuse to permit such visitation, when requested, its exemption from taxation shall thereafter cease and be determined.

Sec. 8. No person shall keep any swine, in any pen or other enclosure, or shall keep, or suffer to be kept, any other nuisance, within one hundred feet of any school-house, or within one hundred feet of any fence enclosing the yard of any such school-house.

Sec. 9. In the construction of this title, except in the construction of chapter sixty and sections six and seven of this chapter and section twenty-two, chapter fifty-six, the word town shall include the city of Providence only so far as to entitle said city to a distributive share in the public money, upon making a report to the commissioner in the same manner as the school committees of other towns are required to do.

Sec. 10. The public schools in said city shall continue, as heretofore, to be governed according to such ordinances and regulations as the proper city authorities may from time to time adopt.

Sec. 11. No superintendent or school committee of any town, or any person officially connected with the government or direction of the public schools, shall receive any private fee, gratuity, donation or compensation, in any manner whatsoever, for promoting the sale or the exchange of any school-book, map or chart in any public school, or be an agent for the sale or the publisher of any school text-book, or be directly or indirectly pecuniarily interested in the introduction of any school text-book, and any such agency or interest shall disqualify any person so acting or interested from holding any school office whatsoever.

Sec. 12. No person shall offer to any public school officer any fee, commission or compensation whatsoever, as an inducement to effect through such officer any sale or promotion of sale, or exchange of any school-book, map, chart or school apparatus.

Sec. 13. All the public schools in the state, including the state normal school, shall be open to the children of officers and soldiers belonging to the state, mustered into the service of the United States, and of those persons belonging to the state, and serving in the navy of the United States, and who died in said service during the late rebellion against the authority of the United States, or who were discharged from said service in consequence of wounds or disease contracted in said service, or who were killed in battle, without any cost or expense for taxes, or other charges imposed for purposes of public education.

Sec. 14. No person shall be permitted to attend any public school in this state as a pupil, unless such person shall furnish to the teacher of such school a certificate of some practicing physician that such person has been properly vaccinated as a protection from small pox, and every teacher in the public schools shall keep a record of the names of such pupils in their respective schools as have presented such certificate.

SEC. 15. Every person violating any provision of this chapter shall be fined not exceeding fifty dollars or be imprisoned not exceeding thirty days, unless herein otherwise provided.

CHAPTER 62.

Of State Scholarships in Brown University.

SECTION 1. The senators and representatives of the several towns shall, from time to time at least once in each year, in grand committee, propose the names of young men of the several towns, of proper age and character, and who shall not have the means of obtaining an education for themselves, as candidates for state scholarships in Brown University, on the foundation provided by the act of congress, approved July second, one thousand eight hundred sixty-two, donating land for the benefit of agricultural and the mechanic arts, in accordance with a resolution passed at the January session, one thousand eight hundred sixty-three, assigning to Brown University the land scrip granted by the United States to the state of Rhode Island for the establishment of an agricultural college.

SEC. 2. The secretary of state shall receive the names of all persons propounded in grand committee as candidates for state scholarships pursuant to the preceding section, and shall record the same in a book to be kept in his office for that purpose; and the governor and secretary of state, acting with the president of the university, shall, on or before commencement day in each year, and as often in each year besides as occasion may require, select from the persons so propounded in grand committee, persons to fill the vacancies then existing in said scholarships; and they shall make such selection in such manner that the people of the several counties shall, from time to time, participate in the benefits of said national donation as nearly as may be practicable, in proportion to their respective population, according to the then last census of the United States.

CHAPTER 63.

Of the State Census.

SECTION 1. A census of the population, manufactures, agriculture, fisheries and business of the several towns shall be taken as they exist on the first day of June, one thousand eight hundred eighty-five and every tenth year thereafter.

SEC. 2. The information obtained by each census shall include all that was obtained by the state census in the year one thousand eight hundred seventy-five, together with such additional information as may be deemed necessary by the census board hereinafter named.

SEC. 3. At least six months previous to the date for taking the census in each census year, the governor shall appoint a superintendent of the census, who, together with the governor and the secretary of state, shall constitute the census board, which shall have the charge of taking the census.

SEC. 4. The superintendent of the census, acting under the advice of the census board, shall prepare and print all the necessary blanks for taking the census, with full and minute instructions to the agents to be employed, and shall distribute the same at least one month before the first day of June in the census years. The superintendent of the census shall also superintend the taking of the census, and receive the returns when completed. He shall also make up the tables from the returns, and prepare and present to the general assembly a report on the census, showing the information obtained and its application to the promotion of the interests of the state.

SEC. 5. The census board shall appoint the agents to be employed in taking the census in the several towns, the preference being given to those nominated and recommended by the town councils of each town, unless on examination they shall be found to be incompetent or unsuitable persons; and the agents employed shall complete their labors and make their returns to the superintendent of the census, on or before the fifteenth day of July in the census year.

SEC. 6. The census board may employ special

agents to obtain information required by the census whenever in their opinion the information can be obtained in this way more correctly and with greater economy to the state.

SEC. 7. If the superintendent, or any other person employed under the provisions of this chapter, shall wilfully neglect to perform the duties required by it, he shall be fined not exceeding one hundred dollars; and in case of such neglect or incompetency the census board may remove any such person and appoint another in his place; and if any person shall refuse to give the information required to be obtained by the provisions of this chapter, he shall be fined not exceeding two hundred and fifty dollars.

SEC. 8. The census board may fix the amount of compensation to be paid to the superintendent of the census not exceeding one thousand dollars, and the compensation of agents and other persons employed under the provisions of this chapter, and the general treasurer shall pay the several amounts so fixed, upon the order of the governor.

TITLE XIII.

OF CERTAIN STATE CHARITIES.

CHAPTER 78.

Appropriations for the Education of Indigent Blind, Deaf and Dumb, Idiotic and Imbecile Persons.

SECTION 1. The sum of six thousand dollars annually is appropriated out of the general treasury, for the education of the indigent blind of this state, at the Perkins Institution for the blind at South Boston, Massachusetts; for the education of indigent deaf mutes of this state at the American Asylum at Hartford, Connecticut, or at the State School for the deaf at Providence; and for the education of such indigent idiotic and imbecile persons of this state, at institutions now established, or that may be established within or without the state, for the education and improvement of such idiotic and imbecile persons.

SEC. 2. The governor may select such indigent persons, being inhabitants of the state, as he shall deem proper as state beneficiaries, and may determine the amount of said appropriations to be applied to the education of each; so that no one person shall receive any portion thereof for more than five years, nor shall any state beneficiary at said American Asylum or at said State School for the deaf, receive more than one hundred and seventy-five dollars; at the Perkins Institution for the blind more than three hundred dollars; and at any other institution more than one hundred dollars, in any one year.

Sec. 3. The governor may draw upon the general treasurer, from time to time, for the purposes aforesaid, his drafts therefor not to exceed in the whole in any one year the amount appropriated in section one of this chapter.

Sec. 4. The governor may draw upon the general treasurer for whatever sum of money he may deem sufficient, not exceeding the sum of twenty dollars yearly in any one case, for the purpose of furnishing necessary clothing to any one of said beneficiaries.

TITLE XX.

OF THE DOMESTIC RELATIONS.

CHAPTER 169.

Of Masters, Apprentices and Laborers.

SECTION 21. No minor under the age of twelve years, shall be employed in or about any manufacturing establishment, in any manufacturing process, or in any labor incident to a manufacturing process.

SEC. 22. No minor under the age of fifteen years shall be employed in any manufacturing establishment in this state unless such minor shall have attended school for a term of at least three months in the year next preceding the time when such minor shall be so employed; and no such minor shall be so employed for more than nine months in any one calendar year.

SEC. 23. No minor who has attained the age of twelve years, and is under the age of fifteen years, shall be employed in any manufacturing establishment more than eleven hours in any one day, nor before five o'clock in the morning, nor after half past seven o'clock in the evening.

SEC. 24. Every owner, employer, or agent of a manufacturing establishment, who shall knowingly and wilfully employ any minor, and every parent or guardian who shall permit or consent to the employment of his or her minor child or ward, contrary to the provisions of the preceding three sections, shall forfeit twenty dollars for each offence, to be recovered before the justice court in the town in which such child shall reside, or in which the manufacturing establishment in which such child shall have been employed shall be situated, one-half thereof to the use of the complainant, and one-half thereof to the use of the district school of the district in which such manufacturing establishment shall be situated, or, if in the city of Providence, to the use of the public schools of said city.

SEC. 25. Every such complaint shall be commenced within thirty days after the offence complained of shall have been committed, with right of appeal as in other criminal cases.

TITLE XXX.

OF CRIMES AND PUNISHMENTS.

CHAPTER 241.

Of Offences against the Public Peace and Property.

SECTION 7. Every person who shall wilfully interrupt or disturb any town or ward meeting, any assembly or people met for religious worship, any public or private school, any meeting lawfully and peaceably held for purposes of moral, literary or scientific improvement, or any other lawful meeting, exhibition or entertainment, either within or without the place where such meeting or school is held, shall be imprisoned not exceeding one year or be fined not exceeding five hundred dollars.

CHAPTER 242.

Of Offences against Private Property.

SECTION 45. Every person who, wilfully and maliciously or wantonly and without cause, writes upon, injures, defaces, tears or destroys any book, pamphlet, plate, picture, engraving or statue, or any other property belonging to any law, town, city, or other free public library, or suffers any such injury to be inflicted while said property is in his custody, shall be fined not less than one dollar nor more than ten dollars, the same to be for the use of the library.

SEC. 46. Every person who shall take or borrow from any law, town, city or other free or public library any book, pamphlet, paper or other property of said library and who, upon neglect to return the same within the time required and specified in the by-laws, rules or regulations of the library owning the property, has been notified by the librarian or other proper custodian of the property that the same is overdue, shall upon further neglect to return the same within two weeks from the date of such notice, be considered to have unlawfully converted the property of the library to his own use. A written or printed notice, given personally or sent by mail to the last known or registered place of residence, shall be considered a sufficient notice.

PUBLIC LAWS.

PASSED SINCE THE PUBLIC STATUTES, FEBRUARY 1, 1882.

CHAPTER 291.

An act to establish a State School for the Deaf.

SECTION 1. The state board of education are hereby authorized and directed to establish and maintain a day school for the education of the deaf and semi-deaf children of this state.

SEC. 2. This school shall be open for the education of any deaf or semi-deaf resident of this state without cost; while residents from other states may be admitted upon the payment of such tuition rates as may be fixed by the board of education.

SEC. 3. In order to equalize the benefits of this school, the board of education may pay the travelling expenses of such indigent pupils, residing in this state, as they may deem advisable, provided that the whole amount thus expended shall not exceed five hundred dollars annually.

SEC. 4. The state board of education are hereby authorized to draw their orders on the general treasurer for the support and maintenance of said school for the deaf, to an amount not to exceed three thousand dollars in any one year.

CHAPTER 316.

An act making an appropriation for the R. I. School of Design.

SECTION 1. The sum of five hundred dollars is hereby annually appropriated to the Rhode Island School of Design.

SEC. 2. The above sum shall be paid by the general treasurer upon the orders of the state board of education, who are hereby empowered and authorized to visit and examine said school at their pleasure.

SEC. 3. The directors of the above named School of Design shall make an annual report to the state board of education in manner and form prescribed by said board of education.

SEC. 4. The state board of education are hereby authorized and empowered to elect two of their number, who, by virtue of said election, shall be members of the board of directors of said School of Design.

SEC. 5. All acts and parts of acts inconsistent herewith are hereby repealed.

DECISIONS.

In the following pages will be found, so far as it has been possible to collect them, a digest of decisions which have been rendered since the establishment of the present school system, both by the commissioners of public schools and by the Supreme Court, which interpret the school law and unfold the principles of its application.

A great many of them were made by the late Hon. E. R. Potter, formerly Commissioner and more recently Associate Justice of the Supreme Court, to whose deep interest in the subject of public education it is in great part owing that the present law was enacted, and whose very intimate knowledge of the design and bearing of the law eminently qualified him to give authoritative opinions concerning it.

In those cases which were published in full in the two preceding manuals, it has been deemed best in this edition to print only the conclusions and the reasons therefor, so far as they were given; but in cases decided since 1873, the plan of giving a fuller statement of the case has been followed.

These decisions will be found arranged topically according to the subjects of the several chapters of the School Law, together with cross references in cases where the decisions cover two or more distinct subjects.

It is sincerely hoped this exposition of the law will be found adapted to the needs of the various school officers of the State and that it will tend to a vigorous enforcement of its varied provisions, and thus to a more healthy and efficient system of public schools.

POWERS OF DISTRICTS AND SCHOOL OFFICERS.

DECISION No. 1.

The district has power, with approval of committee, to open a second school, provided that there be money enough in the treasury to the credit of the district to pay for both schools.

E. R. POTTER, C. P. S.

1851.

DECISION No. 2.

School District No. 10, North Kingstown.

School-house may not be used for any purpose other than those directly connected with public education.

The case involves the right of the district or trustees to use the school-house for other purposes than an ordinary school, and depends partly upon the provisions of the general school laws, and partly upon the conditions of the deed of the lot upon which this particular school-house stands.

The following remark upon this subject is made in the notes to the school act: "A school-house, built or bought by taxation on the property of the district, should not be used for any other purpose than keeping a school, or for purposes directly connected with education, except by the general consent of the tax-paying voters."

The rule here laid down is believed to be substanstantially correct and sound. The district holds the property in trust for educational purposes. The money has been taken from the tax-payers by force of law for certain purposes, and for those only, and cannot be applied by either district or trustee to any other use.

I am of opinion that under the school law the house may be used for educational purposes collateral to the main purpose, such as meetings of the district for school business, lectures upon literary or scientific subjects, debating societies for the people or children of the district, etc. It may not be easy in all cases to draw the line between legal and illegal cases, but it would be perfectly clear that the district could not use the house for trade or religious meetings if any person objected to it.

The question then arises, whether the deed in the present case varies the rights of parties from what they would be if the deed contained no conditions.

By the deed from Joseph Case and others, dated October 11, 1848, the school-house lot is conveyed to the district "for the purpose of maintaining thereon a district school-house and appurtenances, for the benefit of the district school of said district, and for no other use or purpose whatever, except religious meetings," and it is provided "that when said lot of land shall cease to be occupied for the purposes of a district school aforesaid, the same shall revert to the grantors, their heirs and assigns forever."

The exception in regard to religious meetings may be left out of consideration in the present case. It cannot affect it in any way. If the district have no right to religious meetings there, independent of the deed, the deed cannot give it to them. And if the district would have such a right otherwise, it may admit of question whether a provision in a deed would deprive them of it.

Leaving out of consideration the words, "except religious meetings," the remainder of the first passage quoted from the deed appears to me, on the maturest reflection, to express no more and no less than the school law according to the construction herein given to it, would have expressed without the deed; the provision in the deed is exactly in the spirit of the law, and neither adds to nor lessens the rights and powers of the district or trustees.

If the first passage quoted from the deed does not vary the rights of the district from what they would be, if there was no such provision in the deed, the latter proviso appears for the same reason to contain no limitation as to the use of the house, which would prevent its being used for the purposes for which I have said the law, apart from the deed, would authorize.

E. R. POTTER, C. P. S.

I have carefully considered of the above opinion and approve of the same. I have also consulted with Judges Haile and Brayton, who concur with me in opinion.

R. W. GREENE, C. J. S. C.

1853.

DECISION No. 3.

School District No. 12, Burrillville.

A vote of a school district to tax cannot be rescinded after a lawful contract has been made under it.

The fact of the tax being assessed, or of its having been approved by the committee, would not take from the district the right to rescind it. The whole turns upon the question whether a contract was legally entered into under the vote of the district, and I am of opinion that it was. The district, therefore, could not rescind it after the contract was made, without being liable to a suit for damages or to a process like that now applied for.

It becomes, therefore, unnecessary to decide whether the notice for the second meeting was sufficient to justify the district in rescinding the tax.

As a general rule, it is not advisable for district officers to proceed in expending money or making a contract unless they are satisfied that a majority of the tax-payers, absent as well as present, are fairly in favor of it. A mere accidental majority occasioned by absence of opponents is unsafe. And if a case should arise where district officers should undertake to avail themselves of such an accidental majority, and there should be any appearance of a design to anticipate or prevent a repeal of the tax by entering into a contract before there could be time for having another meeting, the commissioner of public schools would not lend the aid of his office to the enforcement of it, but would leave the parties to their action at law.

In the present case, however, there is no evidence but that the trustee acted fairly and honestly.

The proper process must therefore be issued for assessing and collecting the tax according to the before-mentioned provisions of the law.

E. R. POTTER, C. P. S.

1853.

I approve of the above decision.

R. W. GREENE, C. J. S. C.

DECISION No. 4.

School District No. 7, Burrillville.

1. A district may rescind a vote ordering a tax, and postpone the payment of it.
2. A district may borrow money and give a note.
3. Costs of suits in court against a district must be paid by the district.

The question is presented whether a district having voted a tax according to a particular town valuation, can rescind the vote, postpone the payment, and hire the money upon a note of the district.

I cannot see any objection to the right of a district to rescind a vote ordering a tax and postpone the payment of it. The object and effect may sometimes be to include property and persons afterwards coming into the district. Whoever comes into a school district becomes a sharer in all the advantages of the school and district property. If, by their coming, an addition to the school-house is made necessary, such new comers or new property do not pay the whole expense of such addition: the former inhabitants and property have also to pay a portion, and, sharing in all the advantages of former taxation, it does not seem unreasonable that the new property should also share in the burdens. In the present case the school-house was probably built larger than would have been necessary if it had not been expected that there would be an addition to the population of the district.

Any creditor of the district who may be injured by such postponement has a remedy provided by law.

As to giving notes, a district has the undoubted right to make contracts for certain purposes, upon which contracts they may be sued and the debt and interest recovered of them. A note given to such a contractor would be only additional evidence of his claim. And there seems to be no legal objection to the district hiring money of a third person to pay a just debt contracted for purposes authorized by law. This has been the construction always put upon the law in practice, and it appears to me sound.

An objection is also made to costs and attorney's fees. The costs of court in a suit decided against the district must of course be paid by the district. And the reasonable charges of an attorney for defending the suit are proper to be allowed. But services rendered by an attorney to any person in contests with other persons in the district about district business must be paid for by the person for whom they are performed.

Objection is also made to allowance of compound interest. This could not be recovered of the district at law, but I see no objection to the district's agreeing to pay it, and paying it if they see fit, as it would be in the power of the school committee to prevent any excess or abuse of the right.

I therefore confirm the vote of the committee approving of said tax.

E. R. Potter, C. P. S.

1853.

DECISION No. 5.

School District No. 3, North Providence.

1. A person who has the legal qualifications may vote in district meetings even though his name is not on the town voting list.
2. A district has no right to build on a lot till it has a legal title to that lot.
3. Registry voters may vote to ask division of a district.
4. The power to divide a district lies with the school committee.
5. A district should not make a contract to build till a lot has been secured and the plan approved.

It appears from the statement and admissions of the parties, that a meeting duly notified was held August 17th, to reconsider all action relating to building the house, etc. At this meeting a motion was made to rescind the former proceedings, and as declared by the moderator, the vote stood 22 to 22, and the motion was declared rejected. It is admitted that five who voted for rescinding, and five who voted against it, had no right to vote. It is contended that Asa M. Allen, who voted for rescinding, had no right to vote. He was a resident and owned real estate, and according to previous decisions he had a right to vote without his name being on the town registry. A certificate is produced from the assessors to show that Charles Leonard and Crawford Martin, two who voted against rescinding, are not taxed for real or personal property. Of course, not being liable to pay a portion of the tax, their votes should have been rejected. The vote, therefore, stands seventeen for rescinding and sixteen against rescinding, and the votes for building, etc., were legally rescinded.

This of course disposes of all questions relating to

building, but the following points were made and argued, and therefore, to prevent further agitation, I give my opinion upon them.

I am of opinion that a district has no right to build upon a lot until they have acquired a legal title to it, either by lease, deed, or by taking it by process of law. And in the latter case, either the time for appeal to the Court of Common Pleas should have elapsed or the appeal have been decided. The latter caution is necessary because the jury on appeal have a right to alter the location or wholly reverse all the proceedings.

It has been previously decided that a district has no right to take a deed of a house for religious purposes.

If the question of the propriety of dividing the district be proposed in district meeting, registry voters have a right to vote, because it merely amounts to an expression of opinion, and the whole power to divide rests with the school committee to whom the vote of the district is a mere recommendation to be weighed according to its deserts. And registry voters can by law vote upon all questions except taxing or expending money.

It was also contended that the location must be made, a lot legally procured, and the plans approved before a contract can be legally made to build. In the present case the contract was made first. The question is a most important one, because, if a district proceeds before these things are done, it would often lead to a wasteful expenditure of the district's money, if the lot was not procured or the proceedings approved of, and also because innocent parties who contract to build may suffer in consequence. In regard to claims of contractors against building committees or districts, those cases must of course be decided by the courts of law; but I think it is the duty of the school committees and school commissioner to guard against a wasteful expenditure of money by a district majority in all cases where they can do it, and it may frequently be in the power of the commissioner to do it on appeal. And it seems to me plain (without undertaking to decide how innocent third parties may be affected by their acts,) that neither the district nor its officers have any right to make a contract until the lot is fixed and procured and the plans approved of.

The appeal was also made from all doings of the committee in relation to dividing the district; but I do not see anything upon which the commissioner can act. The committee merely decided that the district had not asked to be divided. They did not reject the application. Any individual has a right to petition the committee for a division, and it would be matter of discretion in the committee to adopt or reject it.

E. R. Potter, C. P. S.

1854.

DECISION No. 6.

Joseph O. Clarke vs. School District No. 7.

A school district may borrow money upon the note of the district.

The facts material of this case are these:

That this school district contracted debts to a considerable amount, in building a school-house, and for other school purposes, and for expenses incurred in certain actions and suits in which the district was concerned, which debts, it was conceded, the district was in law bound to pay; that instead of levying a tax on the ratable property of the district to raise the money for the payment thereof, the district hired of the several individuals named as payees of the promissory notes, declared upon in this action, for the purpose of paying said debts with the money borrowed; that the said promissory notes were given by the district for the money so borrowed, and that the money borrowed was applied to the payment of said debts.

The question was raised, whether these promissory notes are valid and binding upon the district, or are void; whether a school district has power to raise money by borrowing, for the payment of its debts lawfully contracted, and to give its promissory notes therefor.

A corporation may bind itself by a negotiable promissory note or bill of exchange for any debt contracted in the course of its legitimate business; that is, in any matter which is not foreign to the purposes of its creation.

A school district (a corporation under the school act) by giving its promissory notes for moneys hired to discharge debts, incurred in the building of a school-house, and otherwise in so doing was not contracting debts in a matter foreign to the purposes of its creation; and the provision of the school act giving this class of corporations power to raise money by taxation, cannot be construed to forbid a borrowing of money for a legitimate purpose.

G. A. Brayton, A. J. S. C.

1855.

DECISION No. 7.

The same person may hold the office of clerk and

that of either treasurer or collector, but the same person cannot be *both* treasurer and collector.

S. AMES, C. J. S. C.

1863.

DECISION No. 8.

School District No. 8, North Providence.

A call for a meeting signed by a *de facto* trustee is valid.

In appeal of Waterman B. Angell and others from acts of trustees in calling the meetings of said district held on the 18th and 27th of June.

The facts upon the point at issue were these. At the annual meetings of said district for the years 1862, 1863 and 1864, as appears by the clerk's record, Ralph P. Devereux, Charles A. Boyd and Henry Armington were successively elected trustees. It was contended by appellants and admitted by respondents that Charles A. Boyd was not at the time of his election eligible (Art. IX, Sec. 1, Constitution of R. I.) to the office of trustee, he being a certificate voter, and by the Constitution (Art. II, Sec. 1,) entitled to vote for general officers only.

It was also contended that a school district must elect either one or three trustees (Title X, Ch. 61, Sec. 5, Revised Statutes,) and in this case, inasmuch as the district had decided to elect, and did elect, *three* trustees, only *two* of whom were eligible, the *third* not being qualified to hold the office, therefore all the acts of these trustees were void.

It did not appear that there was the slightest suspicion, during the entire period for which said Boyd had held the office of trustee, either upon the part of the voters of the district or of the trustees, that he was not a legal and legally elected officer, or that he acted otherwise than in good faith. It has been decided that "a person by *color* of *election*, may be an officer *de facto*, though indisputably ineligible." Ames and Angell on Corporations, Ch. IV, Sects. 9–10, pp. 100–103; also Ch. IX, Sect. 4, pp. 272–5.

I am therefore of opinion that the said Charles A. Boyd, though ineligible to the office of trustee, was by *color* of *election*, *de facto* one of the trustees, that his office was *voidable* only and not *void*, and that the acts of said trustees in calling the meetings held respectively on the 18th and 27th of June, 1864, and from which appeal was taken, were legal and binding acts.

J. B. Chapin, C. P. S.

1864.

Approved. S. Ames, C. J. S. C.

DECISION No. 9.

A district has no right to expend the money of the coming year.

E. R. Potter, A. J. S. C.

1868.

DECISION No. 10.

In cases of temporary absence, declining or refusing to serve, or misconduct, unless the declination or refusal is in writing, or capable of positive proof, reasonable notice should be given to the officer to appear and show cause why the office should not be declared vacant.

E. R. Potter, A. J. S. C.

1873.

DISTRICT MEETINGS.

DECISION No. 11.

In the election of a committee to purchase land for site of a school-house which has been approved according to law and the price of which is known to the meeting at the time of making such appointment, and in the election of a building committee for the building of that which has been lawfully approved, the moderator may receive the vote of any resident of the district, who is at the time qualified to vote in town meeting for town officers.

H. BARNARD, C. P. S.

1848.

Approved. R. W. GREENE, C. J. S. C.

DECISION No. 12.

It is the duty of the moderator to put all questions to vote.

E. R. POTTER, C. P. S.

1848.

DECISION No. 13.

For a secondary school, the school committee call the first meeting, and the trustees call the others.

E. R. POTTER, C. P. S.

1849.

DECISION No. 14.

School District No. 3, North Providence.

Omissions in the records of school officers may be supplied on proper evidence.

Evidence to correct or supply omissions in the records of school officers, I think may properly be admitted. In the case of clerks of districts, it seems absolutely necessary, as they are often unacquainted with the forms of doing business. In the case of a school committee, however, the presumption is stronger that they are competent men, and will be careful to see that their record is well kept. Yet even here great mischief might result from excluding all evidence other than the record. But it should be received with great caution, as after any considerable length of time parties might not recollect it alike.

E. R. POTTER, C. P. S.

I approve of the above decision.

R. W. GREENE, C. J. S. C.

1853.

DECISION No. 15.

School District No. 3, North Providence.

1. Qualifications of voters in district meetings. | 2. Residence of voters.

The question turns upon the legality of the votes of Finigin and Heaton, which had been struck off by the school committee, and were not examined by Mr. Potter.

It appears in evidence that Finigin is a naturalized citizen, and a resident in said district; that he has owned real estate sufficient to qualify him to vote since September 4, 1850; that his naturalization papers are dated March 4, 1851, and that he is taxable in the town, and is liable to be taxed in the district for the house in which he lives. It was contended that, his name not being on the town voting list, he could not, for this reason, be allowed to vote in district meetings. The qualifications for voting in district meetings are identical with those for voting in town meetings, with the same proviso as to voting upon any question of taxation. (See act relating to public schools, sec. 32.) But the restriction which forbids the moderator to receive the vote of any one whose name is not on the voting list, (see act relating to elections, sec. 26,) is not contained in the school laws as a restriction to voting in district meetings. A moderator is therefore bound to receive and count the vote of a person who is a citizen and a holder of real estate in a district, whenever he has resided in it a sufficient length of time, even if his name is not on the voting list. Such is the opinion of the late commissioner of public schools, in decision number 5, given on the case of Asa M. Allen, who claimed a right to have his vote restored, after it had been annulled by this same decision of the school committee.

In the case of Heaton, it is testified, that he became of age on the 28th of December, 1853, that he holds undivided real estate to a sufficient amount to qualify him to vote, and that he is a resident in said district. It is objected that, prior to August 17, 1854, he removed into Massachusetts, and thus lost his citizenship in Rhode Island. In opposition to this it was proved that he went into Massachusetts for a merely temporary purpose, and that he never intended to change his abode, and that his estate, his business, and his real home, remained in Rhode Island. It appears to me that the principles which ought to govern in deciding questions of domicil or residence, as laid down by Judge Story in his Conflict of Laws, and quoted in Appendix No. 9, to the Report of the Commissioner of Public Schools for 1854, would render Heaton, still a citizen and a voter in district meetings in Rhode Island, since his intention of only temporary removal seems plain.

It is, therefore, my opinion that the votes of Finigin and Heaton, ought to be counted as against said motion to rescind. The vote will then stand seventeen ayes, eighteen nays; and the motion is lost. The several votes of the district relating to building are therefore still unrescinded, and of the same force and validity as if such motion had not been made.

ROBERT ALLYN, C. P. S.

Approved. G. A. BRAYTON, A. J. S. C.
1854.

DECISION No. 16.

A qualified voter, if he be not a property holder, is eligible to office.

E. R. POTTER, C. P. S.

1854.

DECISION No. 17.

School District No. 3, North Providence.

Registry voters have the right to vote on the question of the propriety of dividing the district.

If the question of the propriety of dividing the district be proposed in district meeting, registry voters have a right to vote; because it merely amounts to an expression of opinion, and the whole power to divide rests with the school committee, to whom the vote of the district is a mere recommendation to be weighed according to its deserts; and registry voters can by law vote upon all questions except taxing or expending money.

E. R. Potter, C. P. S.

1854.

Approved. R. W. Greene, C. J. S. C.

DECISION No. 18.

School District No. 3, North Providence.

All business of special meetings of school districts must be specified in the notice of the meeting.

The commissioner is of opinion that an election of trustees at a special meeting, the notice whereof did not specify that business, cannot be considered valid. Section 29 of the school law enacts that notice of the time, place, and *object*, of every special meeting shall be given for five days inclusive, before the holding of the same. The notice put up on the 1st for a meeting to be held on the 6th, contained no specification concerning the election of a trustee; and as this meeting was adjourned, and another notice was posted up, it must be held that the meeting of the 15th was not competent to elect a trustee—an item of business not named in the original warrant. If it is said that a motion was made to accept the resignation of Trainer, and this being postponed to the next meeting was a sufficient notice of the intention to elect a trustee, it will be an ample reply to say that such postponement cannot be considered a notice according to the requirements of the law. For section 30 of the school law specifies the mode of notice, which is "by publishing in some newspaper, or by putting up notice, or in such manner as the school committee may require." The notice certainly was not given in any of these three ways. It may also be said, that if the law requires the business of every special meeting to be named in the warrant, trustees, if so disposed, might prevent action on any necessary matter by failing or refusing to insert it as an item in the warrant calling the meeting. But section twenty-seven of the school law, provides against this by commanding the trustees to call a meeting to be held "within seven days, on the written request of any five qualified voters, stating the object for which they wish it called," and if the trustees neglect or refuse to call such meeting the school committee may call it and fix the time of holding it.

R. ALLYN, C. P. S.

1856.

Approved. GEO. A. BRAYTON, A. J. S. C.

NOTE—The law concerning the time of notices for district meetings has been changed since the above decision.

DECISION No. 19.

School District No. 7, Burrillville.

1. No person to vote on any proposition to raise a tax, unless he is liable to pay a part of said tax.
2. To change a vote of a district it must be shown that enough illegal votes were cast to change the result.

The commissioner decides that the school law does imperatively prohibit any person from voting on any question concerning taxation, unless he has paid, or shall be liable to pay, a portion of such tax; and on examination of the names of persons who voted for and against said motion to pay the debts of the district with this money, he finds that no person so having paid a portion of said tax, voted in the affirmative, and that five persons so having paid a portion of said tax, voted in the negative. He, therefore, declares that the motion was lost.

R. Allyn, C. P. S.

1856.

DECISION No. 20.

School District No. 2, Cranston.

Any resident of a school district, qualified at the time as a registered voter to vote in town meeting, is entitled to vote in the district meeting to assess a tax for the repair or improvement of the district school-house, provided he be liable on account of his personal estate to contribute to the tax for which he votes, although he has never been assessed for such personal estate, and his name is not upon the last list of town voters.

Appeal to the commissioner of public schools, from the vote of a district meeting of school district No. 2, Cranston, ordering a tax of $500 to be assessed upon the ratable property of the district, for the purpose of repairing and improving the school-house in said district.

By the statement of facts, it appears a vote was passed at a district meeting held on the 21st of May, 1859, by eighteen affirmative, against sixteen negative, votes ; and the appellants contested the validity of the order of assessment by impeaching the right to vote, at said meeting, of Horatio N. Randall and Charles O. Bennett, residents in said district, both of whom voted in the affirmative. It further appears from the statement that Randall was in September, 1858, assessed in the town of Cranston for town taxes, the sum of $3.65 upon real estate valued at $1,200, which he paid to the town collector on the 8th day of March, 1859 ; and that having, in January or February, 1859, sold his real estate, he was in July of that year, assessed for town taxes in Cranston, the sum of $1,07½ upon personal estate valued at $500—the same estate for which he was assessed for his proportion of the tax in question. Bennett's name, though upon the registry, was not upon the list of voters of the town of Cranston, prepared for the April or June elections, 1859.

By Sec. 8, Ch. 62, of the Revised Statutes, every resident in a school district is entitled to vote in a district meeting, who is qualified at the time to vote in a town meeting, with this further restriction,—that to vote upon any question of taxation of property, or of expenditure of money raised thereby, he must either *have* paid, or *be liable* to pay, a portion of *the* tax. He need not, however, be upon the last list of town voters ; since such lists are not prepared or made up for district, as they are for town meetings; and there is, therefore, no mode provided by which he could get upon the list, however well qualified he might be at the time to vote.

In this view of the statute, it is plain, that Randall was entitled to vote for the tax ordered to be assessed by the district meeting of school district No. 2, of Cranston, held on the 21st day of May, 1859. Though not upon the town voting list made up for the April election, 1859, he was qualified, as a registered voter, to vote at the meeting in question, by the payment of a tax to the amount of a dollar, upon property valued at a sum exceeding one hundred and thirty-four dollars, assessed within the year next preceding, and more than four days prior to the time of his voting (Rev. Stat. Ch. 22, Sec. 1; Ch. 23, Sec. 14), and although he had parted with the real estate upon which *this* tax had been assessed, he was, on account of personal estate to the amount of $500, liable to contribute to, and therefore entitled to vote for, the school district tax in question.

S. Ames, C. J. S. C.

1859.

DECISION No. 21.

I am satisfied no particular length of residence is necessary in a district to entitle a person to vote, provided it be *bona fide*. This was formerly held so, and I cannot see any good reason to doubt it.

E. R. Potter, A. J. S. C.

1872.

DECISION No. 22.

Right of a husband to vote on his wife's real estate.

1. Any husband who married his wife previous to December 2, 1872, and whose wife acquired the property on which he claims the right to vote previous to December 2, 1872, is entitled to vote under Art. II, Sec. 1, if he is otherwise qualified and if the property is a freehold estate of the value prescribed in the constitution, whether he has had children by his wife or not.

2. Any husband married since December 2, 1872, or whose wife has acquired the property on which he claims the right to vote since December 2, 1872, is entitled to vote under Art. II, Sec. 1, if he is otherwise qualified and if the property is an estate of inheritance of the value prescribed in the constitution, provided he has had issue by his wife capable of inheriting it,—but otherwise, not.

T. DURFEE,
W. S. BURGES,
E. R. POTTER,
C. MATTESON,
J. H. STINESS,
Supreme Court.

1878.

DECISION No. 23.

Emma A. French vs. School Committee of Coventry.

1. **District meeting held under but *one* notice is illegal, even though all the voters knew of the meeting.**

2. **Neglect of duty by a school officer renders him liable to a penalty, but does not invalidate a school.**

This was a case where a trustee was elected at a

meeting called by only one notice, whereupon objection was made and the old trustees called another meeting by posting two notices, at which meeting another party was elected trustee than at the first meeting. The trustees elected at the second meeting, hired the appellant, who proceeded to teach the summer term of school; the trustee elected at the first meeting having in the meantime surrendered possession of the school-house. The school committee, however, from doubts as to the legality of the trustees election, refused to recognize the school, though notified of its existence by the teacher according to their rules; and at the end of the term they refused to draw an order for the payment of her wages, though the proper return, duly signed, was presented.

It was decided, First, that an election held at a meeting called by but *one* notice was invalid, that verbal or parole notice cannot be accepted in place of the plain statutory requirement of *two* written notices. Second, that the failure of the school committee to recognize a school, which was otherwise legal, could not be construed into a condemnation of such school. Third, that the failure of a school officer to visit a school, or to give notice as required by law renders the *official* liable for neglect of duty, but does not destroy the legality of the school.

T. B. STOCKWELL, C. P. S.

1875.

Appealed to Supreme Court and decision sustained.

E. R. POTTER, A. J. S. C.

1881.

See Decision No. 5 Page 75.
See Decision No. 8 Page 79.
See Decision No. 10 Page 80.

DISTRICT TAXES.

DECISION No. 24.

The approval by the committee of a tax legally voted, cannot be appealed from.

H. BARNARD, C. P. S.

1844.

Approved. E. R. POTTER, C. P. S.

1854.

DECISION No. 25.

Committee may rescind their approval of a tax before contract has been entered into.

E. R. POTTER, C. P. S.

1853.

DECISION No. 26.

The bondsmen of a town collector are not liable for his acts as district collector.

E. R. POTTER, C. P. S.

1854.

DECISION No. 27.

School District No. 14, Smithfield.

1. Votes as to times for assessing or collecting a tax are directory merely and do not prevent the action being taken subsequently.
2. Real and personal estates must be kept separate in all assessments of taxes.
3. It is sufficient if a tax is approved by the school committee before the warrant for collection is issued.

A direction to assess or collect a tax within a specified time is directory merely, and if, by accident or otherwise, it is not done within the time fixed, it may be done within a reasonable and convenient time afterwards.

The law positively requires real and personal estate to be assessed in separate columns, and any assessment made otherwise is illegal.

Although it is prudent to procure a tax to be approved by the school committee before any proceedings are had under the vote, yet it is sufficient if the tax be approved before the warrant is issued to collect it.

E. R. POTTER, C. P. S.

Approved. R. W. GREENE, C. J. S. C.

1854.

DECISION No. 28.

School District No. 8, North Providence.

Commissioner cannot compel trustees to grant a warrant for the collection of a tax, and must not interfere to perform their duties.

A tax was voted, assessed and partly collected; and the commissioner is now asked to appoint a collector and to issue a warrant to collect the balance.

Counsel for a tax-payer in said district opposed to the granting the petition raised a question of jurisdiction, and moved that the petition be dismissed because the commissioner had not power to grant the relief prayed for.

After consideration, the commissioner submits the following as his decision on the question of jurisdiction:

It is seriously doubted whether, under the forty-sixth section of the school law,—the section cited as giving all the authority over the case,—the commissioner has power to order and enforce the collection of the balance of a tax legally voted, approved, assessed, and partly collected by a district under the rightful authority of their trustees. The case contemplated by that section appears to be one in which there is no power in the district to collect taxes and thus satisfy any just claims which creditors may have against it; and not one in which the power has already been exercised to a certain extent, and the officers of the district are simply indisposed to proceed. The petition does not allege any errors in the assessment nor any want of power to collect, but only asks the commissioner to perform a duty legally devolving upon their officers, but very repugnant to their feelings; or, in other words, it is but asking one officer of the state to undertake a duty where his authority is at least doubtful, and discharge it for another where the latter's power is far more clear.

Besides, it seems that according to the sixty-sixth section of the school law, the trustees of the district have a right to presume that the tax was a legal one, and that it is, therefore, properly and lawfully due, inasmuch as there appears to have been no exception taken to the vote by which it was ordered, nor to the act by which it was assessed.

It is a principle which must govern the commissioner, that he will not encroach upon the powers, prerogatives, or duties of any officer below him elected by the people themselves. And as the trustees of the district were elected for this very purpose of collecting all lawful taxes, and as they have ample powers and securities, the petition is therefore dismissed.

R. ALLYN, C. P. S.

1855.

DECISION No. 29.

School District No. 7, Scituate.

A district tax cannot be paid to any other person than the collector.

Where Y's land had been levied upon and sold by a tax collector for non-payment of a school district tax, and Y. brought ejectment against the purchaser, alleging and offering to show that prior to the levy and sale he had paid his tax to the treasurer of the district. *Held* that evidence to this effect was inadmissable; that the tax collector is the only officer authorized to collect a tax assessed by a town or school district: and that the levy and sale was valid.

It is by law made the duty of the district collector to collect the tax and pay it over to the treasurer or his successor in office. To him is delivered the tax bill and warrant for that purpose. He gives bond for the proper performance of that duty if a bond is required, and is entitled to the commission provided by law for his services in collecting the tax. He must collect the tax and pay it over to the treasurer within the time specified in his warrant. If he fails to do this he may be sued or prosecuted for his default. The treasurer has no authority to collect the tax; but only to receive it of the collector when collected, and disburse it according to law. He does not have the tax bill for the purpose; and payment to him is no more a legal payment than it would be if made to any other officer of the district, who is not authorized by law to collect the tax.

A. Bosworth, A. J. S. C.

1855.

DECISION No. 30.

Case of Edward S. Wilkinson, guardian, in appeal from tax in District No. 1, North Providence.

1. Imperfection of a district clerk's record does not render invalid a tax properly voted.
2. A vote to assess by percentage is not illegal.
3. The assessment of a tax will be legal if it is clear to whom and on what property it is assessed.

Upon the facts as presented and after considering the arguments of the parties, and after advising with Judge Brayton, of the Supreme Court, the commissioner is of opinion that the imperfection of the records of the clerk will not affect the legality of the tax. The proceedings, so far as the notice of the meeting and the form of the resolution are concerned, were undoubtedly legal and proper. As to the mode of levying the tax by percentage instead of by specific sum, the commissioner is not aware that this is contrary to the school law. It is evident that the school committee might approve a specific sum after the tax had been assessed by the trustees; and as there is no evidence to show that the committee did not approve some specific sum, it must be held that the failure to vote a specific sum, does not render the whole tax invalid. Also in reference to the assessment of the tax to Edward S. Wilkinson for Nathan Lazelle, instead of to Edward S. Wilkinson, guardian for Nathan Lazelle, since it was shown that this had been the mode of assessing taxes on the said Nathan's personal property in the town of North Providence, and since it was not shown that the said Wilkinson had ever experienced any difficulty in the settlement of his accounts with the said Nathan's inheritance before the court of probate, the commissioner does not deem it to be proper for him to interfere, and solely on this account decree a forfeiture of the tax on the part of the district. This is a matter of technical law and he does not therefore attempt to settle the meaning and usage of that law. It is deemed just and best that in this case, this tax should follow and be paid as other taxes have been paid.

R. ALLYN, C. P. S.

1856.

DECISION No. 31.

School District No. 7, Warwick.

A district tax can be confided to a town collector when there is a district collector duly appointed and qualified.

I decide, that, according to the 37th section of the act relating to public schools, "Any district may vote to place the collection of any tax or rate bill in the hands of the collector of town taxes," notwithstanding there be a district collector; and I, having been satisfied by evidence that a vote to that effect has been passed at a regular district meeting of School District No. 7, of the town of Warwick, decide that the collection of the tax in question may be legally confided to the collector of town taxes of that town.

R. ALLYN, C. P. S.

1856.

I approve of the above decision.

S. AMES, C. J. S. C.

DECISION No. 32.

School District No. 11, Exeter.

1. A tax approved by the school committee if subsequently increased, must be again approved.
2. A trustee not authorized to insure a school-house without authority from the district.

Three points of objection can be sustained. The "notice" of the second meeting, the approval of the school committee, and the insurance. The "notice" and "insurance" may be reduced to one. The power to insure a school-house is by Sec. 3, Chap. 61, School Law, vested in the district and not in the trustee. Yet if the "notice" had specified insurance as one of the objects of the meeting, a vote of the district sanctioning the trustee, would have been legal.

It is my opinion and decision that this tax is not legal,—because the whole tax has not been approved by the school committee, and the notice not sufficient to authorize the district to sanction the act of the trustee in procuring insurance on the house.

J. KINGSBURY, C. P. S.

1858.

Approved. S. AMES, C. J. S. C.

DECISION No. 33.

The excess of a tax beyond the district's indebtedness does not affect the legality of tax.

J. B. Chapin, C. P. S.

1859.

DECISION No. 34.

If taxes are paid to the treasurer, the collector will have the same claim to his percentage as if the taxes had been paid to him originally.

J. B. Chapin, C. P. S.

1860.

DECISION No. 35.

In the case of a person, who resides in a district only a part of the time, the question of taxation of personal property must depend upon the time that said person resides in the district.

J. B. Chapin, C. P. S.

1860.

DECISION No. 36.

When there is only one tax paying voter in the district his vote is sufficient to order a tax.

E. R. Potter, A. J. S. C.

1868.

DECISION No. 37.

School District No. 4, Middletown.

1. In any appeal where a district as such is an interested party, the district must be officially notified of the hearing.
2. Where a tax is assessed by assessors appointed by the commissioner they must give notice of their assessment and proceed to value the property independent of the town valuation.
3. A tax collector acting under an apparently legal warrant would not be liable for damages in case it was proved defective.

In this case the trustee made a contract with the teacher, and this contract was made known to the district meeting, and the vote of the district thereon (though invalid for other purposes) may well be held to be a ratification of it.

Subsequently upon the district refusing to carry out the terms of the contract, the teacher, Coggeshall, and the trustee, Carpenter, united in an appeal (which we may construe to mean that they applied under this provision) to the commissioner May 12, 1870, and he appointed the same day for a hearing, and it is alleged that "due and actual notice of such hearing before the commissioner was given, and both parties were present." It is not alleged to whom notice was given, or who were present; and by both parties, we must understand the two persons before named, no others being either directly or indirectly referred to. The district was the party against whom the contract was to be enforced, and of course a proper party to this proceeding, but as the plea does not allege that the district was notified, we must infer that it was not, and that omission was fatal.

It is also alleged that the commissioner, on July 9, 1870, decided that the tax voted by the district, "sufficient to pay the residue of the contract," should be assessed and collected in accordance with the power conferred by Revised Statutes, R. I. cap. 64, § 4; and issued a warrant to Messrs. Peckham, Carpenter, and the district clerk, to assess a tax "on the valuation of the town assessors of 1869–70," and appointed the district collector to collect it; that the district clerk declined to act as assessor, and notified the commissioner; and the commissioner (whether verbally or in writing is not said) directed the other two to proceed and assess the tax; and that they were legally appointed and qualified, and did assess a tax on said valuation, etc., etc.; that the commissioner approved it, and, August 30th, issued his warrant to said Wm. F. Peckham to collect it.

When a district trustee apportions a tax, he is to do it (Revised Statutes R. I. cap. 64, § 2,) on a valuation made by the town assessors. But when a tax is to be collected under the commissioner's warrant, the assessors may use the town valuation as a guide; but they must, after all, assess it upon their own judgment. And it being an actual assessment, proper notice should have been given, which is nowhere alleged.

The collector, acting under an apparently legal warrant, would not be held liable as collector.

E. R. POTTER, A. J. S. C.

1877.

DECISION No. 38.

School District No. 19, South Kingstown.

1. School commissioner has no power to order a tax in a district except in cases where the law specifically provides for such a case.

2. School commissioner cannot approve a district tax, hence there is no appeal to him in such matters, except as to questions of its formalities and illegalities.

In this case school district No. 19 of South Kingstown voted a tax for school purposes and the school committee of the town refused to approve of it. From that refusal an appeal was taken to the school commissioner, and on the hearing it was objected that the school commissioner had no jurisdiction to reverse the committee's vote and to approve of the tax himself, and as requested by the party he has laid the case before one of the judges for his decision.

The right of appeal given by Chapter 55, Sec. 1, of the School Law, is expressed in very general terms. Yet it is evident that it cannot be construed to authorize him to reverse the proceedings of the Board of Education, and so of some other officers who have duties to perform under the law. So if a district refuses to order a tax, *he* can only order a tax in the case provided for by law, where a contract has been made, etc. To hold otherwise would be to make the school commissioner the absolute dictator on questions of taxation.

We must be guided in deciding this question by the intention of the law so far as can be gathered from its language and history, and we may also resort in cases of doubt to the practical construction of it as settled by usage and previous decisions.

It is obvious that the commissioner may on appeal reverse a vote of a district or committee for informality or illegality, in many cases where he would not have a right to make any further or new decision of his own. This would be carrying out the object of the law in giving the appeal, which has always been held to be the prevention of litigation, by furnishing a cheap and speedy mode of deciding on such informalities and illegalities.

The location of school-houses is one of those questions where the object of the law is to guard against the prevalence of mere local interests, to guard the interests of minorities and of non-resident owners of property; and in these cases the commissioner has always from the very beginning of the system and with the presumed acquiescence of the legislature, exercised the right to make a new location on appeal; And so in many other cases, where it may be necessary to protect the rights of teachers and scholars from the consequences of local excitements and quarrels.

The principal difficulty in the present case grows out of the very different language used by the General Assembly in Chap. 48, "Of the powers of school districts," Sects. 3 and 4. The difference is too marked to be overlooked, and I must therefore conclude that while the commissioner may reverse, or refuse to reverse, a vote or decision of the committee in such a case as the present one, for illegality or informality, he cannot make a decision approving the tax.

E. R. POTTER, A. J. S. C.

1877.

DECISION No. 39.

School District No. 1, Richmond.

1. In case of assessing tax where a town assessor is to be called upon, the trustee before calling upon him, must endeavor to agree with the parties as to their valuation.
2. The school committee's records, and not the town clerk's, are the ultimate authority as to a district's boundaries.
3. An assessment of a greater amount than that voted by the district is illegal, whether the excess be great or small.

In the matter of the appeal of the Wood River Branch Railroad against school district No. 1, of Richmond, it was claimed by the appellant that a certain tax assessed by the trustee of said district in accordance with a vote of the district, of November 3, 1878, was illegal and void. 1st. Because the trustee called upon a town assessor to value that portion of the railroad's property lying in the district, without trying first to secure an agreement with the corporation. 2d. Because the records of a district's boundaries as recorded in the town clerk's office are the legal bounds and the ultimate authority on that question, while in this case the trustee followed certain bounds which were furnished by the school committee. 3d. Because the vote to levy the tax only authorized a tax of $125, whereas the tax as assessed by the trustee amounted to $125.40.

Upon the first point raised by the appellant I am of the opinion that the trustee should, after the tax was voted, have endeavored to agree with the railroad corporation, before calling upon the assessors for their aid. Such is the natural and only legitimate meaning of the proviso, "if unable to agree with the parties interested," which occurs in the section under which the action complained of was taken. Moreover, no such proviso existed in the school law of 1845; but it was subsequently inserted, evidently because it was found by experience that a change was necessary in that direction.

The second claim of the appellant I do not think is sustained by the law. In the section of the law which refers to the town clerk keeping the records of the district boundaries, nothing is said or implied which makes them the final authority. On the other hand, the school committee is explicitly given full power over this question of district boundaries.

In regard to the legality of an assessment where the total amount assessed is greater than the amount voted by the district, I think there can be no doubt that it is illegal. The right to exceed the prescribed amount at all, implies the right to carry the excess to almost any amount, and hence, in fact, transfers the power of determining the amount of the tax from the district to the trustee.

T. B. Stockwell, C. P. S.

1879.

I hereby confirm the above decision.

E. R. Potter, A. J. S. C.

DECISION No. 40.

School District No. 4, West Greenwich.

1. Where school committee change territory from one district to another, with an agreement of the owners that they are willing to be set back when the committee think best, such agreement is a waiver of notice of such action by the committee.
2. Property that has never contributed to the erection of a school-house ought not to be relieved from such responsibility.
3. Change of boundaries does not alter or destroy the identity of the district.
4. Property added to a district after a tax is voted, is liable if it is in the district at time of assessment.

From the evidence submitted it appears that in February, 1876, the appellants being then located in district No. 4,-West Greenwich, petitioned to be set off to district No. 10, because at that time there was no school-house in district No. 4, and therefore their school privileges were very poor; and unless they belonged to district No. 10, if they availed themselves of the school there, they would be liable to pay for it. They were accordingly set off to district No. 10 by the committee; upon the understanding as confessed by both parties, that whenever district No. 4 should build a school-house this property should contribute its regular quota thereto, it never having been assessed for this purpose.

Matters continued thus till the spring of 1879 when the question of building a house was agitated in district No. 4, and finally at a meeting held March 24, 1879, the district voted to build and also to assess a tax of $350 to defray the expenses.

The house was constructed during the summer and fall of 1879, and in November, when the question of raising the money to pay for the building arose, the trustee before making the assessment of the tax applied to the school committee for a particular statement of the bounds of the district and for such a correction of the lines as would restore to the district the property previously transferred to district No. 10.

Accordingly a meeting of the committee was called for November 29, 1879, when the matter was discussed and finally laid upon the table till the next meeting, December 4.

One object of the postponement was to give notice to these two parties of the proposed action, but through some misunderstanding no such notice was given, and on said December 4 the committee met and passed the vote appealed from.

On the 5th of December the trustee made out his rate bill of the tax voted as above on the 24th of March, and delivered it to the town collector for collection.

The appellants claim a reversal of this vote of the school committee because;

First. No notice of the proposed change was given them.

Second. They had no voice in laying or voting the tax which is now assessed against them.

Third. It is more convenient for them to be in district No. 10 than in district No. 4.

To these claims the respondents rejoin that

First. It has never been the custom in this town to give parties notice of intended changes in the boundary lines of districts, nor is such notice called for by the statutes.

Second. The action of the committee was simply carrying into effect the original understanding that when district No. 4 built a school-house this property should contribute its quota.

Third. The school-houses in the two districts are not far from being equidistant from these two farms in question, while the approaches to each are such as to render a choice between them very difficult to make. Certainly no preponderating advantages exist in favor of district No. 10.

Fourth. The amount of taxable property is much less in district No. 4, than in district No. 10 ; hence the latter ought not to be enriched at the expense of the former.

After a careful examination into the facts I am of the opinion that the decision of the school committee in question should be confirmed for the following reasons :

First. The original boundaries of the districts are thus re-established. It is quite safe for us to assume that the original division into districts was the fairest distribution that could be made, so far as the rights of all were concerned.

For the transfer of this property from district No. 4 to district No. 10 to be made permanent, would be to the very manifest injury of district No. 4, and would require for its justification very strong reasons which I fail entirely to find.

Second. The acknowledged understanding between the appellants and the school committee at the time of the transfer from district No. 4 to district No. 10 constitutes a practical waiver of notice; the act complained of being virtually the second part of an agreement previously made.

Third. The property in question having never contributed to the erection of a school-house should be so assessed, and it is very clear that district No. 4 is the district entitled to the benefit thereof.

Fourth. I am fully of the opinion that the best interests of the two farms in question will be full as well, if not better, promoted by their being joined to district No. 4, than if they were annexed to district No. 10.

The claim that the tax is not collectible of the appellants because it was voted before they were joined to the district and therefore a tax in which they had, and could have had, no voice, is not tenable, because the district which voted the tax and the district which assessed it were legally one and the same district, and all rights and powers which were vested in the one, were of necessity vested in the other. If such were not the case, every time the bounds of a district were changed it would be necessary to re-elect officers and re-enact any votes passed previous thereto which were intended to have any farther force or validity. It is difficult to see, therefore, how the trustee when he came to assess the tax which had been voted by the district could do otherwise than assess *all* property which the district contained at the date of his assessment.

To the claim that such a decision violates the principle that one cannot be assessed for a tax which he had no voice in ordering, it is sufficient to say that protection against any injustice is secured by the provisions for an appeal, as in this case, on the question of merit in the change of bounds.

I do therefore confirm and establish the vote of the school committee of December 4, 1879, whereby the farms of Gideon Bailey and Clark R. Franklin were joined to district No. 4, West Greenwich; and also the validity of the taxes assessed upon said property by the assessment of December 5, 1879.

T. B. STOCKWELL, C. P. S.

1881.

Approved. C. MATTESON, A. J. S. C.

TRUSTEES.

DECISION No. 41.

The loss of the qualification as elector required to render a trustee eligible to the office, would not cause a forfeiture of the office.

E. R. Potter, C. P. S.

1849.

DECISION No. 42.

When no appeal from the manner of the election of trustees is taken within a reasonable time, if they act in this capacity during the year, their acts as such are valid, and they are the acting trustees of the district.

E. R. Potter, C. P. S.

1849.

DECISION No. 43.

When three trustees are elected, each must be elected every year.

E. R. Potter, C. P. S.

1851.

DECISION No. 44.

When from neglect of trustees, the school committee assume the power of opening a school, the trustee is bound to respect their orders.

E. R. POTTER, C. P. S.

1851.

DECISION No. 45.

School District No. 5, Little Compton.

A trustee of a school district can only be removed during his term of office for cause.

I am of opinion that a district having once legally made an election of any of the officers required by law to be elected, would have no right to rescind it.

The case would be different, however, with persons who were merely appointed by the district as a committee for some particular purpose. Over such cases the district would have complete control, and might remove such agents at pleasure.

A trustee once elected and accepting could only be removed for good cause and after notice and hearing. The contrary doctrine would lead to continual contests and confusion.

E. R. POTTER, C. P. S.

1853.

DECISION No. 46.

School District No. 2, North Providence.

1. **Trustees can hire at whatever wages they please.**
2. **The legal school year begins May 1st, annually.**
3. **Trustees have no power to reduce a teacher's wages or to dismiss him during the term for which he is hired.**

At the proper time of the year, and under the approbation of the school committee, the trustees have unlimited authority to employ a teacher at whatever wages they please. If they employ at very high wages, they may, by a vote of the district, assess and collect a tax to defray the extra expense. If they employ at cheap wages, the unexpended balance of their appropriation must be divided among the other districts. And if trustees choose to use only a part of their share of the "teachers' money" for their own district, and leave the remainder to other districts, thereby providing an inferior school for their own children and a better one for their neighbors, no power is known to prevent, provided they do it at the proper time. At such times as trustees may lawfully hire teachers for their schools, they may hire as cheaply as they can, provided the school committee will approbate those hired.

In reference to the time when the legal school year commences, there can be but one opinion. In absence of any vote of the district prescribing the time at which the teacher's contract shall terminate, and in the absence of any written or specific agreement between the trustees and teachers as to this time of terminating the contracts, and in such districts as have established permanent or yearly schools with fixed terms and vacations, the legal school year must be settled by the statute. Section 21 of the act relating to public schools, makes it necessary for a district to keep a school not less than four months at some time during the year ending on the first of May, in order that it may be entitled to draw its portion of the "teachers' money" for the year thereafter ensuing; the commissioner is required by section 2, annually in May to apportion the money annually paid out of the general treasury for public schools among the several towns according to law, and his office annually expires on the second Tuesday of that month. Section 20 enacts, among other things, that the school committee "shall apportion as early as practicable in each year, among the districts, the money received from the State;" and section 21 further provides "that at the end of the school year any money which shall remain unexpended may be divided by the committee among the districts the following year;" and finally, section 26 makes it the imperative duty of a district to hold its annual meeting near this time, namely, in April or May. From all this and from the fact that the returns of the districts to the school committees and from the committees to the commissioner are made to this date, and the district officers are elected for the year ending at the annual meeting, when their terms of office expire unless continued by special statute, the commissioner must decide that the legal school year begins on the first of May annually, or by section 26, in cases there provided for, at the time of the annual district meeting, and in the absence of all proof of any specific vote of the district, or of any specific agreement between the trustees and Mr. Willard, that the contract for salary was from the time of the annual meeting held on May 29th, 1855; and that the payment of two months' salary after that time was a virtual renewal of the agreement for another year, and should so be held in common justice and honesty, unless, for reasons good and sufficient, the school committee of the town should dismiss him, as they have a right to do under the 56th section of the school law.

As to the general power claimed by the trustees to

reduce a teacher's wages, or in the alternative to dismiss him from their school, and that on a very brief notice, it should be remarked, that the school law manifestly intends that the State shall have some charge of all the schools which it in part supports. It therefore very properly forbids trustees to hire as teachers persons who do not possess certain moral and literary qualifications—and even those who possess these in an undoubted degree, unless they hold or can obtain a certificate in the required form and signed by the proper authorities. The law aims to prevent trustees from retaining a teacher who neglects his duty, and provides that the school committee may dismiss such an one. All these guards seem to be reared in order to prevent the trustees of a school district from doing two things which would necessarily tend to destroy or degrade their school; from employing the immoral or incompetent, and thus poisoning or stinting the morals and the minds of the children, and from hastily dismissing the worthy teacher by reason of any private or personal pique, or in consequence of some temporary excitement. And as the State furnishes a portion of the money which supports the public school of every district, and gives that district all the right it has to exist, and to collect taxes for the further support of its schools, it is but proper that it should step in by its officers and prevent the trustees from injuring the school, or from suddenly discharging or reducing the compensation of a teacher against whom no deficiencies are alleged. It is believed that such powers as are claimed would materially injure any school, and that under the school law they are not conferred upon the trustees.

1855. R. ALLYN, C. P. S.

DECISION No. 47.

Case of Philip B. Stiness, Jr., vs, J. H. Willard, Clerk of School Committee, North Providence.

1. Teachers cannot hold over end of school year without agreement to that effect, special or implied.

2. Clerk has no authority to perform of his own motion acts that are discretionary with the committee.

The commissioner's opinion upon the first point whether these teachers, employed as they must have been on a new term commencing within one of the months fixed for the annual meeting — say April 28th — were legally employed, is, that these teachers were not legally employed. The time of the annual spring vacation in these schools comes within the month of April, a month in which the annual meeting of the district may occur. This must be reckoned the end of their year, unless by special or implied agreement. There was a vacation, and the trustees, or the school committee, are the only authority to regulate the length of that vacation, and consequently one or the other of these bodies must fix the beginning of the term after that vacation. The trustees could not have done that legally, for they had no legal meeting during the time from March till May 27th, or about that time. And the school committee did not fix the time of commencing these schools. The teachers must, therefore, be considered as having begun the schools of their own motion, and they were, therefore, not legally employed in such sense as to be entitled to orders on the town treasury for teachers' money for their wages. It may here be remarked, that as the time from April 28th to May 31st was only a small portion of the summer term, there was ample time for an election of trustees by the district, and the adoption of these schools both by these trustees and the school committee, but at the time of ordering these bills they had not thus been adopted.

As to the second point, whether the clerk could legally order bills of this kind, the commissioner is clearly of opinion, in accordance with a decision of the late commissioner, Hon. E. R. Potter, that the clerk has no power whatever to do any act that is discretionary with the committee to do or not to do. It is a well settled principle that such a body as a school committee cannot delegate to any one of its servants any discretionary power. It may, and indeed will, often find it necessary to delegate ministerial powers, but it cannot go further than this in its acts of delegation. As these bills were under protest, and as it lay wholly in the discretion of the school committee to receive the schools and visit them and allow the teachers their bills for wages, in short, to make them legal, it must be held that any act of the clerk which would attempt to forestall the action of the committee in regard to that protest would be illegal and void.

R. Allyn, C. P. S.

1856.

DECISION No. 48.

School District No. 8, West Greenwich.

1. Districts have no power to hire teachers by vote.
2. District trustees must act as a board.

The commissioner decides that a district, at a meeting of its voters, has no power to hire a teacher even if the meeting is legally called, and such an item is inserted in the warrant. In sections 33–36, inclusive, of the act relating to public schools, which enumerate the powers of districts, no mention is made of the "power to employ" teachers; but, on the contrary, section 40, specially confers upon the trustees that power, and it is made "their duty" "to employ one or more qualified teachers for every fifty scholars in average daily attendance." It is, therefore, the plain duty of the trustees to employ all teachers, and a meeting of the voters of a district could only be advisory.

As to the mode in which the trustees shall discharge their duty, it ought to be a rule never to be departed from, that when the district appoints three trustees, as it may, the three should meet and confer upon all questions relating to their official duty. Many of their duties are deliberative, and, therefore, cannot be delegated to, or assumed by, any one of their number; such as making contracts with teachers, or for repairs or fuel and preparing tax lists; and these things, of course, require a meeting of the three, or at least of a majority after due notice given to the absent minority. And it is highly improper, that any single one should, in any duty not strictly ministerial and prescribed to him by vote of the body at a meeting, act with the expectation that his colleagues will ratify what he shall have done.

The mode of notifying meetings of trustees is not specified by law, and is therefore left to be a matter of common agreement among them. Generally, as they are near each other, a verbal notice from the chairman, will be sufficient.

R. Allyn, C. P. S.

1856.

Approved. G. A. Brayton, A. J. S. C.

DECISION No. 49.

If a district vote to build or repair a school-house, and appoint a building committee for that purpose, and the building committee be empowered by general terms as "to build" or "repair" as distinguished from merely *contracting* for the same, that is, be armed with general powers to carry through the project of the district, such powers would include as incidental, the power to give orders on the district treasurer for the payment of those employed by them.

If, however, the power of the committee be so restricted by the form of the vote as to exclude, or not naturally to include this power, then it belongs to the trustees of the district, in whom is the general custody, in the sense of care, of the property of the district, and who are expressly armed with all powers necessary to carry out the powers and duties of the district.

S. Ames, C. J. S. C.

1858.

DECISION No. 50.

School District No. 2, Cranston.

If a district elect one trustee at annual meeting, they cannot at a subsequent meeting elect two more.

My decision is that the vote and proceedings of the district at their meeting held May 7, 1859, are void.

At the annual meeting, the district could elect one trustee or three trustees, as they might decide. They decided to elect and did elect but one,—Mr. Richardson. There was thus an election at the annual meeting, and the trusteeship of the district was full, according to the authorized decision of the district. There was, therefore, no election of trustees to be made at any subsequent meeting.

As no vacancy in the office has occurred from any of the causes named in Chap. 61, Sect. 5, of the Revised Statutes, there was none for the district to fill, at their adjourned meeting of May 7, 1859.

Mr. Richardson is, therefore, the sole trustee of school district No. 2 of the town of Cranston, for the year ensuing his election.

S. Ames, C. J. S. C.

1859.

DECISION No. 51.

School District No. 1, Barrington.

A school-house may be occupied for a singing school, when such occupation does not interfere with the ordinary school, without the consent, or even against the vote, of the district.

The question at issue is manifestly without the jurisdiction of the district, and has already been decided upon by the proper tribunal, viz: by the commissioner of public schools, approved by the Chief Justice of the Supreme Court.

With regard to the instance cited in said appeal, the use of the house for a singing school, as a violation of such decision, I am of opinion that the use of said house for such instruction is perfectly legitimate "to purposes connected with public instruction."

Instruction in vocal music is a part of our system of public education, and is so recognized and paid for by the city of Providence out of the "teacher's money," and is recognized and employed as an important element of education in nearly all the rural districts of our commonwealth. Many of our school committees insist upon its introduction into the public schools, and nearly all the school reports which reach the office are emphatic in its recommendation. And certainly if the younger children may be instructed in vocal music in the public school-house, and this too during school hours, there can be no legal objection why their older brothers and sisters and friends may not receive such instruction at the same place out of school hours.

Nor is the fact that the teacher receives pecuniary compensation from his pupils pertinent to the question; for to allow it to be so would be to question the legal use of school-houses for public schools, many of the sessions of which are prolonged by *private* subscriptions, and are of course kept, in the same sense in which the one is kept to which reference is made, by "private" individuals.

The manner in which any teacher is paid, or whether his services are gratuitous, does not affect the question in point. Moreover, such a legitimate use of the school-house would not require "the general consent of the tax-paying voters," said "private individual" having permission for occupancy from the trustees of said district, in whom the law places the custody of the school-house.

J. B. CHAPIN, C. P. S.

1860.

Approved. S. AMES, C. J. S. C.

See Decision No. 2, Page 69.
See Decision No. 8, Page 79.
See Decision No. 10, Page 80.
See Decision No. 28, Page 93.

Powers and Duties of School Committee and Apportionment and Uses of School Money.

DECISION No. 52.

School District No. 5, Cumberland.

1. School teacher without a certificate cannot draw "teachers' money."

2. No particular mode of notifying meetings of the school committee.

1st. No teacher can, under any circumstances, be entitled to demand any portion of the public money unless he has a certificate of qualification valid at the time he keeps the school.

2d. Although the committee may provide by by-law a mode of calling meetings of their body, such by-law would not exclude any other mode of calling meetings; and if a quorum be present, and all those who are capable of attending have had reasonable notice, and there is no charge of any unfair or improper proceedings, the meeting will be held to be a legal one; the committee being a body appointed by law for the performance of a trust, and the law itself prescribing no particular mode of calling such meeting.

E. R. Potter, C. P. S.

1849.

Approved. R. W. Greene, C. J. S. C.

DECISION No. 53.

The town has a right to *direct* how the money it raises shall be divided, and the committee must apportion it accordingly, but the town can give no order for the payment of any portion of it. Towns can make special appropriations to aid districts, but it cannot be done out of the school money, either State or raised by the town under the school law.

E. R. POTTER, C. P. S.

1850.

DECISION No. 54.

School District No. 3, North Providence.

A school district ought not to be divided when it can conveniently establish a graded school.

I am of opinion that that portion of the proviso contained in Sect. 4, par. 1, of the school act, respecting the grading of schools, is to be construed as laying down a principle for the regulation of the discretion of the committee. It is not definite and positive in its terms, and cannot be made so from the nature of the case. Each case must depend upon its own circumstances. But before acting in such a case the committee should enquire and adjudge that each district will have the required number of scholars, and that the schools cannot conveniently be graded.

In regard to the facts of the case, taking all the circumstances together, and with the probability that the population of the north part of the district from its vicinity to the city must be constantly increasing, and that, therefore, the district presents a favorable opportunity of carrying out, sooner or later, the apparent intention of the proviso, I am of opinion that the district should not be divided, and the decision of the committee is therefore reversed.

E. R. POTTER, C. P. S.

I hereby approve of the decision of the commissioner.

R. W. GREENE, C. J. S. C.

1851.

DECISION No. 55.

The school committee are the proper authority to dismiss a teacher who does not give satisfaction.

E. R. POTTER, C. P. S.

1852.

Approved. R. ALLYN, C. P. S.

1855.

Approved. J. B. CHAPIN, C. P. S.

1861.

DECISION No. 56.

School District No. 3, North Providence.

1. School committee may limit their certificates, but general certificates must be construed to their plain purport.

2. School committee cannot delegate the power to annul a teacher's certificate.

On consideration I adhere to the decision formerly made upon this point, that although the committee have the power to limit their certificates to particular schools, yet if they see fit to give a certificate of general qualification, it must be construed according to its plain purport, and to allow the written certificate to be contradicted or varied by any understanding not expressed on the face of the certificate itself would be a dangerous practice, leading to continual misunderstanding and litigation.

The power of annulling certificates is an important one. It gives the committee control over the teacher, it authorizes them to pronounce a judgment against him for unfitness or misconduct, which may have the effect of ruining him in his profession, and of injuring materially his prospects for general success in life. If the construction was doubtful, these considerations would incline me to lean against the right claimed for the committee to delegate this power. But the construction appears to me to be plainly, that the committee have not the right to delegate.

And if the sub-committee had not the power to annul the certificate, the subsequent recognition of it by the committee would not render it valid.

E. R. Potter, C. P. S.

1852.

DECISION No. 57.

School District No. 3, North Providence.

1. School committee may not compel a gradation of schools.
2. School committee have power to limit and explain their certificates.
3. School committee cannot delegate its general powers.
4. Committee have power to annul certificate for good cause.

1st. The school committee may promote by advice and recommendation, but have no power to compel, a gradation of schools by a district.

2d. The committee have the power to limit and explain their certificates. To construe the law to require perfection in the branches named in section 54, would be unreasonable, and, indeed, it is impossible to make a perfectly definite standard. If so, there is no reason why the certificate should not express the degree of qualification.

3d. The committee cannot delegate their general powers. The powers of visiting schools and examining teachers they are specially authorized to delegate.* There can be no objection, also, to a committee authorizing its officers to draw orders for payment of bills, upon the performance of certain conditions, as on making a return, etc. But to delegate a power, which is supposed to imply the exercise of a discretion in the committee, seems contrary to the intention of the law in giving such power to the committee.

4th. The committee have the undoubted right to annul a certificate, or dismiss a teacher, for good cause. No particular form is necessary for doing this. But the trustee should be plainly informed that the certificate is annulled, or the teacher dismissed. And the teacher should be notified, that he may have a chance to defend himself.

E. R. Potter, C. P. S.

1852.

* By the school law of 1839, the committee were expressly authorized to delegate ALL their powers, and the practice was productive of great evil.

DECISION No. 58.

Appeal from School Committee of North Kingstown.

Scholars cannot be compelled to make fires for school-houses by either trustee or school committee.

The regulation No. 26, adopted by the school committee October 25, 1852, is in these words: "The trustee or trustees of each district, with the teacher, may cause the fires to be made in the school-house, by directing the scholars of a suitable age to take turns in making the fires, or procure them to be made in any other way they may think proper."

In a private school the teacher has a right to prescribe his own terms. The parent who sends children to the school delegates to the teacher the right to govern them according to his own rules, and to punish to a reasonable extent for the violation of them. The remedy of the parent, if he does not like the school or its regulations, is in not sending to it.

Before the establishment of a public school system, all our schools were of this character. The practice of requiring scholars to perform services of this sort was generally adopted in the country schools, and in many of them has continued to this day. It remains to inquire what alteration the establishing of public schools by law, supported by the common funds and property of the State, has made in the rights of the parties in this respect.

To a public school every parent has a legal right to send his children. He sends them subject to the lawful authority of the teacher, and to the lawful regulations which may be prescribed for the discipline and studies of the school, but he has a right to insist that no regulations be made which the law does not authorize.

The right claimed, if it exists at all, must be derived from the general power of the committee to make regulations, or from the authority given to districts and trustees to make assessments on scholars and their parents. (Sec. 59.) The latter, however, it is very evident, contemplates only assessments to be paid in money and not labor.

The power of the committee to make regulations is given by section 1, which authorizes them "to make and cause to be put up in each school-house, or furnished to each teacher, a general system of rules and regulations for the admission and attendance of pupils, the classification, studies, books, discipline, and method of instruction in the public schools."

It seems to me very plain that the power to make a regulation of the character of the one in question is not given in this paragraph. We might as well infer a right to require the scholars to cut and saw the wood. And as I can find no other authority for it in the law, it must be considered as unauthorized by law, and accordingly null and void.

E. R. Potter, C. P. S.

1853.

DECISION No. 59.

School District No. 3, West Greenwich.

School committee have power to so divide town money as to equalize the amounts among the several districts.

In reference to the petition which asks that the commissioner would reverse the act of the committee of said town dividing the public school money equally among all the districts of the town, the commissioner decides that he can afford no relief. The general school law does indeed expressly state, that the one-half of the money given from the general treasury for public schools in any town shall be divided in proportion to the average attendance of scholars in the several schools of the town; and the other half equally among the several districts. But it does not specify the manner in which a town may divide the money raised by its own vote, and that arising from the payment of registry and military taxes. It was given as the opinion of the late commissioner, Hon. E. R. Potter, that towns are at liberty to divide this according to their own pleasure, so that they use it judiciously for the good of their schools. It may follow, therefore, that a town may so divide its own money, and registry and military taxes, as to make up the inequalities in the sums payable to its several districts, that would arise from the legal division of the State's money. And as the usage is of long standing thus to equalize the portions of public money paid to the several districts in West Greenwich, the commissioner sees no reason to disturb it, and feels that he has no authority so to do.

R. ALLYN, C. P. S.

1856.

Approved. G. A. BRAYTON, A. J. S. C.

DECISION No. 60.

John H. Willard vs. School Committee of North Providence.

1. Election of chairman and clerk necessary to the legal organization of a school committee.
2. School committee cannot vacate the office of clerk but by hearing and for cause.

Has the school committee a right, after having made an election of a clerk,—an officer created by the school law and necessary to the organization and legal action of the committee,—to remove that clerk, unless by charges and trial, after notice, for misdemeanor before the expiration of the term of their office?

I am of opinion that the school law, (see sections 9 and 10,) makes the election of a chairman and clerk necessary to a legal organization of the committee, and the law nowhere gives to the committee any power whatever to remove its officers. This removal can therefore only be made for cause, and in the same manner as any other officer elected for a specified time could be removed. This must be by trial, and after notice.

With this view, a decision of the late commissioner, Hon. E. R. Potter, accords. That was in regard to a district trustee, an officer of no more responsibility than a clerk of the school committee, and was to the effect that "an election once made could not be rescinded, and that he, the trustee, could only be removed after notice and a hearing."

My decision, therefore, is, that said vote, passed as it was without previous notice and opportunity given for hearing and trial, is void.

1857. R. Allyn, C. P. S.

Approved. S. Ames, C. J. S. C.

DECISION No. 61.

John H. Willard vs. School Committee of North Providence.

A clerk of a school committee may be removed from office for cause, after notice and hearing.

Mr. Willard in his argument contends that no power is given in the school laws to the committee to remove a clerk, and that such an officer can be removed only by impeachment; but section sixty-five of the law, to which reference is made, speaks of penalties for the non-performance or mal-performance of duties by school officers, and does not mention removal from office. There is a wide difference between removal from office, and punishment inflicted for willful crime in office. As removal is not mentioned in the law, this must, when deemed necessary, be done in accordance with common law. A decision was made by the late commissioner, Hon. E. R. Potter, in relation to the removal of trustees, in which he says, "They can only be removed after notice and trial for cause;" and this implies that these and other school officers can be removed, by the bodies appointing them, after such notice and trial, for cause. An opinion given by Chief Justice Ames on January 31, 1857, is to the purport that a clerk of a school committee can be lawfully removed for good cause, after notice and trial. Another opinion, given by the same judge in case of Smith, asking a rehearing before the commissioner, implies that the evident design of the school law was to relieve the courts from litigation in the small matters that may concern the public schools, and to provide tribunals, cheap, accessible, and speedy, for the redress of wrong or injury in such cases. But if a school committee must be compelled to go before a court of law for redress, in case of every refractory clerk or other officer elected by them, for the sole purpose of giving expression to, or of recording their doings, this very laudable object of the law will be entirely defeated. This seems entirely contrary to the whole spirit of the law, and is believed to be contrary to usage also.

It is therefore held, that the committee have power to remove their clerk, after sufficient notice of their intention, and opportunity for trial and defence. That the appellant had such notice and made defence was fully proved. The appellant asks that the facts may be laid before Hon. Chief Justice Ames for his opinion thereon.

It then only remains to consider whether the causes alleged for removal, as above recited, were true and sufficient to warrant the action of the committee. And the commissioner decides that in his opinion they were fully proved to be true, as above stated, and that they were also sufficient to warrant the removal.

R. ALLYN, C. P. S.

1857.

I fully concur in the above opinion.

S. AMES, C. J. S. C.

DECISION No. 62.

A single estate may not be taken from one town to be united with a district in another town for the purpose of forming a joint district, especially when other estates are as favorably situated for the same purpose.

J. KINGSBURY, C. P. S.

1857.

DECISION No. 63.

A formal recorded vote is not necessary to the location of a school-house.

S. AMES, C. J. S. C.

1859.

DECISION No. 64.

Town money can be used for incidental expenses.

J. B. CHAPIN, C. P. S.

1860.

DECISION No. 65.

The power to expel a pupil from school is in the hands of the committee.

J. B. CHAPIN, C. P. S.

1864.

DECISION No. 66.

Isaac M. Bull et al. vs. School Committee of the Town of Woonsocket.

1. The power to originally lay out or form school districts is vested in the school committee.
2. School committee have the power to discontinue one district, even against its will, and join it to another.

This is an appeal by a number of persons, styling

themselves "residents, tax-payers and voters in the 10th school district of Woonsocket," to the commissioner of public schools, from the decision and doings of the school committee of Woonsocket, the effect of which was to discontinue district No. 10 and to enlarge No. 9, so as to include the territory previously within No. 10.

The commissioner of public schools lays before us a statement of the facts of the case, agreed to both by the appellants and appellees, for our decision. These facts are: "1. The three villages of Globe, Bernon and Hamlet were originally parts of the town of Smithfield, and were each organized as independent school districts. 2. When these districts were set off from Smithfield and annexed to Woonsocket, they retained their original district organization, suffering no change except that of name, the Globe District henceforth being known as No. 8, Bernon as No. 9, and Hamlet as No. 10. 3. At a legal meeting of the school committee of Woonsocket held June 6, 1873, it was voted, that district No. 10 at Hamlet be and it is discontinued; also that the boundaries of district No. 9 be established so as to include what formerly belonged to both Nos. 9 and 10."

The question raised upon these facts by the appeal is, did the school committee have power to discontinue district No. 10 and to alter the boundaries of district No. 9 so as to include the territory previously within No. 10, the voters in these districts having never voted to consolidate them?

Section 3, chapter 53, of the General Statutes provides, that "The school committee may alter and discontinue school districts, and shall settle their boundaries when undefined or disputed; but no new district shall be formed with less than forty children between the ages of four and sixteen, unless with the approbation of the commissioner of public schools." The school committee rely upon this section as authority for their action. It certainly seems sufficient.

The appellants, however, contend that such a construction of the section above quoted is inconsistent with other provisions of the statutes relating to public schools. They refer to section 2, chapter 47, of the General Statutes: "Of the powers and duties of towns . . . . relative to public schools," which is, "Any town may be divided by a vote thereof into school districts," and argue that under the construction claimed, it would be possible for a school committee to nullify the action of the voters of a town. They also refer to section 5, chapter 50, of the General Statutes, "Of joint school districts," by which "any two or more adjoining school districts in the same town may by concurrent vote, with the approbation of the school committee, unite and be consolidated into one district, for the purpose of supporting public schools, and such consolidated district shall have all the powers of a single district," and contend that the construction claimed renders this section practically useless, since if a school committee may first discontinue a district and then enlarge an adjoining district so as to include the one discontinued, a consolidation of the two may be affected by the action of the school committee alone, *without the concurrent votes of the districts;* and a result may thus be accomplished *indirectly* in a manner different from that provided for accomplishing the same result *directly.*

The appellants also refer to chapter 48, of the General Statutes, "Of the powers of school districts," by which school districts are made bodies corporate and vested with certain powers necessary for the discharge of their duties.

The appellants assert that section 3, chapter 53, of the General Statutes should be so construed as to harmonize with these several sections to which they refer, and suggest that all the General Assembly intended was, that school committees should alter and establish the boundaries of school districts when undefined or disputed, and form new districts from parts of districts, when from any cause it should become desirable to sub-divide existing districts, and should only wholly discontinue or abolish a district with its consent.

Doubtless all these provisions of the statutes are to be so construed as to make them consistent and to give effect to all. But is the construction claimed for section 3, chapter 53, really inconsistent with the proper construction of the other sections of the statutes to which our attention has been directed? We think not.

The language of the first of these—section 2, chapter 47—is, "Any town *may be divided*, by a vote thereof, into school districts." This may mean either that the town may divide itself by its vote, or that it may be divided, if it shall so vote. We think, that the true construction is the latter. When a town has voted that it be divided into school districts its power has ceased. It then becomes the duty of the school committee to lay off the districts and define their limits, the only limitation upon their power being, that "no new district shall be formed with less than forty children between the ages of four and sixteen, unless with the approbation of the commissioner of public schools.'' It is true that in the present statute no express authority is given to school committees to *form* districts, but we think it is necessarily implied by the language of this limitation. Some of the obvious reasons for this construction of section 2, chapter 47, are,—

1. The form of the expression is the passive ''*may be divided.*''

2. If the other construction be adopted, there is no limitation upon the power of towns in the formation of districts as to the number of children which such districts shall contain.

3. The districts can be laid off and their limits defined much more intelligently by a body like a school committee than by a town.

4. Our construction is more consonant with the policy of the school laws, which vest the ultimate control and direction of school affairs, subject to appeal to the commissioner of public schools, in the school committees.

A review of the legislation upon the subject of forming school districts confirms the construction which we have adopted.

The second provision of the statutes to which the appellants have directed our attention as inconsistent with the construction claimed for section 3, chapter 53, is section 5, chapter 50. The purpose of this latter section was to enable adjoining districts in the same town, where the compactness and number of the population would warrant, to unite for the purpose of maintaining public schools,—the advantages of which are too apparent to be dwelt upon,—and as an inducement to so unite, section 6 provides, that such consolidated district shall be entitled to receive the same proportion of public money as the districts composing it would receive if not united; but they are not permitted to unite, except with the approbation of the school committee, or, on appeal, of the commissioner of public schools. We do not think that this power of voluntary consolidation conferred upon adjoining districts was intended to prevent the school committees from consolidating two or more districts, if in their opinion the interests of the schools or the judicious use of the public money required it, even though it should be against the wishes of the districts. The right of appeal to the commissioner of public schools would restrain and afford a remedy against the arbitrary exercise of such power by a school committee.

The third ground of objection urged by the appellants to the construction of section 3, chapter 53, claimed by the appellees is that under that construction school committees have power to discontinue school districts without their consent. We do not deem this a valid objection.

By the school laws of Massachusetts, chapter 23, section 24, of the Revised Statutes as construed in *Richards* v. *Daggett*, 4 Mass. 534, and *Allen* v. *School District No. 2 in Westport*, 15 Pick. 35, towns had power, from time to time, to form new districts and to divide or alter the limits of old ones. School districts were also corporations, with powers similar to those of our own. In *School District No. 1 in Stoneham* v. *Richardson*, 23 Pick. 62, Morton, J., in the opinion of the court, says; "But school districts are corporations not only very limited in their powers, but also of precarious existence. They may not only be varied and modified in the extent of their territorial limits, but also annihilated by a body over which they have no control." Again, on page 69, he says: "The power of towns to form new districts at their discretion necessarily implies the power of abolishing the old ones. And as these corporations are brought into existence without the volition of their members, embracing every one within their limits, *nolens volens*, so they may be abolished without the consent and against the wish of all the members."

We think the school committee were authorized to take the action appealed from, and that the appeal should be dismissed.

C. MATTESON, A. J. S. C.

1875.

DECISION No. 67.

Nathan T. Verry vs. School Committee of the Town of Woonsocket.

For general laws to modify special laws affecting particular towns, the modifying intention of the legislature must be clear.

The town council of Woonsocket, June 12, 1878, elected Mr. Verry superintendent of public schools. Afterwards the school committee claimed the right to elect the superintendent, and June 24, 1878, elected Mr.

White. From this vote Mr. Verry appealed to one of the justices of the Supreme Court.

On account of the importance of the question involved, the case was, by request of the justice to whom it was presented, heard before the full court and argued by counsel.

By the act incorporating Woonsocket, Pub. Laws, cap. 666, January 31, 1867, it is provided that the council shall elect so many town officers as by the laws of the State are or shall be required, excepting only a few whose election had been before provided for in the act. It seems to have been the intention of the act to vest in the council, with these exceptions, all the powers of the town in regard to those matters.

The election of superintendent of schools has been at several times regulated by general law. See Revised Stat. R. I. cap. 60, § 5; Pub. Laws, cap. 923, March 24, 1871. And by Gen. Stat. R. I. cap. 47, § 5, now in force, any town may elect, and if it fails, the committee shall elect one. It is compulsory that the town shall have a superintendent, but the committee are to elect if the town does not.

By Gen. Stat. R. I. cap. 31, § 8, it was enacted that "every town . . . shall have and exercise all the powers and privileges . . . conferred upon it by its charter or by the several acts of the General Assembly specially relating to it, until the same shall expire by their own limitation or shall be revoked or repealed."

The present case involves the question how far special laws affecting particular towns are to be deemed to be repealed or altered by general laws, without express mention.

Such cases are not without their difficulties; but while the power of the legislature is undoubted, the intention should be plain. It is obvious that if the legislature should grant to a town a right to do some particular thing, and should afterward enact by general law that no town should do it, there would be no doubt as to the construction. See cases in Dillon Municip. Corp. §54, 2d ed.; Sedgwick Stat. & Constit. Law, 2d ed. 99.

In the present case, under the special act, the powers of the town as a corporation in this respect were to be exercised, not in town meeting, but in town council, and the general law merely enacts that if the town, which does not necessarily imply town meeting, fails to elect, the school committee should elect. On this view there is really no repugnance between the general and special acts.

The town here did through its council elect, and the election by the school committee was therefore illegal, and this vote must be reversed.

As there is nothing in any of the special acts to which our attention has been called prescribing the number or mode of classifying the committee, there can, of course, be no question but that these subjects must be regulated by the General Statutes of the State.

E. R. Potter, A. J. S. C.

1879.

DECISION No. 68.

Uses of the Public Money.

1. Public money may be used for current expenses of the schools.

2. Public money cannot be used for repairs or fixtures to school-houses.

As to the law concerning the uses which may be made of the money raised by the town for school purposes, there is no section or clause which specifically sets forth such uses. A careful comparison however, of two or three different sections of the law will at once convince one of the fact that the law makes a broad distinction between the "support of schools" and the "providing of school-houses, etc." See sections 1 and 3 of Chap. 50 and sections 3 and 4 Chap. 51 of the Public Statutes.

But lest there might be some question, we have had at least two decisions from the highest authority, covering this point.

In 1851, Judge Potter, then commissioner of public schools, decided that no portion of the school money, either State, or raised by town tax for the "support of schools," could be used for the building, furnishing or repairing of school-houses where the district system prevailed.

In 1858, John Kingsbury, commissioner, wrote as follows: "After consulting Chief Justice Ames I must decide that the phrase 'other expenses' in Chap. 64, Sect. 9, Revised School Laws, applies to expenses for things similar to books, fuel, etc. and which do not come under the name of fixtures. I must therefore further decide that window curtains are fixtures."

If reference is made to the law above quoted it will be found to refer to the old rate-bill and the uses to be made of the proceeds thereof. Now since the increased appropriation for the support of schools which the towns were obliged to make when the rate-bill was abolished, was clearly intended to supply the deficiency created by the absence of the rate bill, it is equally clear that the purpose for which this increased appropriation was designed must be identical with those for which the former fund was raised.

In a word it has always been held, whenever the question has been raised, that in any town where the property was owned by the districts, that no part of the appropriation for the support of schools could be used in payment for such district property or any part thereof.

T. B. STOCKWELL, C. P. S.

1880.

DECISION No. 69.

School District No. 3, South Kingstown.

1. The motive or reason which prompts a gift of land or money to a district not a subject of inquiry or appeal.
2. A gift of land or money to a district not contrary to law.
3. The location of a school-house adjacent to one's territory not a grievance within the view of the law.

In the appeal case of C. W. Wilcox from the action of the school committee of South Kingstown whereby they fixed a new location for a school-house in district No. 3 of said town, the following is a statement of the main facts. After several meetings of the district for the purpose of considering the question of repairing the old house and building a new one, at a meeting held September 5th, an offer was received from W. H. Potter to give the district $500, if they would use it to buy a lot, called the Hazard lot, about fifty rods farther north on the same road as the old site. His offer was accepted and the district by a vote of 25 to 10 decided to take that lot and build a new house. The action of the district was reported to the school committee, who met, examined all the sites proposed, heard all parties interested, and finally voted unanimously to locate the new house on the Hazard lot.

The appellant resists the location of the school-house on the new lot because it abuts directly upon his premises and he regards the school-house so near him as an injury, and its location there will entail expense upon him. He also claims, in common with some others, that sufficient reasons do not exist for a change of site, and that, even if they did exist, the proposed site is not a suitable one.

During the hearing the appellant offered evidence as to the character of the motive or purpose which prompted Mr. W. H. Potter to make his offer of $500 to the district, but it was ruled out by the commissioner on the ground that the result of the act, as affecting the interests of the district, and not the motive or cause for it, was the subject of inquiry.

Upon the question of personal inconvenience raised by the appellant, I do not regard the alleged grievance as coming within the scope of the provisions of the law, and it must therefore be set aside.

As to the claim that the gift of Mr. Potter was of

the nature of a bribe and so contrary to law, and the subsequent action of the district, growing out of it, void, I do not so understand either the law or the practice under it. From the beginning of the school system, private parties have continually donated lands and money to towns and districts for school purposes and with specific provisions and conditions, and I have never known it to be held that such gifts were contrary either to the letter or the spirit of the law.

Upon the claim that sufficient reasons do not exist for a change of site and that the proposed site is an unsuitable one, I am of the opinion that a change is needed, and that the Hazard lot is, under the circumstances, a fit and suitable lot and one that will tend to promote the best interests of the district. I do therefore approve of the action of the school committee, and confirm their vote whereby they located the proposed new school-house on the so-called Hazard lot; and the appeal is dismissed.

T. B. STOCKWELL, C. P. S.

1881.

Approved. C. MATTESON, A. J. S. C.

DECISION No. 70.

Case of Appeal of John Nevins vs. School Committee of Cranston.

1. A change from one edition of a text-book to another edition of the same book, not a "change" of text-books.
2. The notice of the proposed "change" required by law does not include a specification of the particular book to be introduced. It is enough to state the *kind* it is proposed to *change*.
3. Notice must be given at a regular meeting of the committee, but action may be taken on the question at any subsequent meeting, provided proper time has elapsed since the notice.

The facts appear to be as follows: In 1880 the agent of Warren's geographies visited the several members of the school committee of Cranston with reference to the introduction into the schools, of their revised, or N. E., edition, as it is called. After interviews with all of the committee, the chairman of the committee ordered of the publishers, Messrs. Cowperthwait & Co., a lot of the N. E. edition, which were sent to him with authority to put them into the schools at what are called exchange or introduction rates. No minute however appears on the records of the committee of any action by them relative to this matter.

After the receipt of these books, the chairman notified part of the schools, and possibly all, that the pupils could change their geographies in accordance with the terms as given to him. But in no case were the pupils compelled to make this change; it was left optional with them and the teacher.

At the regular meeting of the school committee, January 9, 1882, the following written notice of a proposed change in geographies was given by Mr. J.

A. Latham, one of the committee: "Notice is hereby given the school committee that the matter of changing the text-books upon geography be considered at some future meeting." Upon the records of a special meeting, held February 4, 1882, the following minute appears: "The notice in relation to Harper & Bros'. geography was brought forward and action thereon deferred till next meeting."

At the adjournment of this meeting, February 11th, the following action on this subject was taken.

Voted, "That it is advisable to adopt Harper & Bros'. geographies for the use of the public schools of this town."

It is from this vote of the school committee that the appeal is taken, and the appellant claims its illegality and asks for its reversal and overthrow for the following reasons:

First. Because the introduction of Warren's N. E. edition in 1880 was a change in text-books within the meaning of the law, and therefore no further change can be made until the expiration of three years from the date of that change.

Second. That the notice under which the vote complained of was passed, was given at the previous meeting which was not a regular meeting.

Third. That the notice, which it is claimed was given at the regular meeting, January 9th, was not sufficiently definite, either as to time or nature of the proposed change, to conform to the requirements of the law.

Fourth. That the vote adopting Harper's geographies was passed at a special meeting, whereas it is the intent of the law that such action shall be taken at a regular meeting.

To these points the respondents aver:

First. That no change in the eye of the law was made by the committee in 1880; but a simple arrangement was made for giving to the schools the advantage of a newer book of the same kind.

Second. That the written notice submitted by Mr. Latham at the January meeting, as appears from the records, was the notice under which the committee acted.

Third. That said notice was as definite as the law requires.

Fourth. That the statutes do not require action upon the adoption of text-books to be taken at a regular meeting, and hence the matter is subject to the control of the committee.

I am of the opinion: First. That no change in text-books was made by the committee in 1880. It is certain that no legal change was made, as no record exists of any such action, nor is there any claim that the committee ever took action as a body on that question. But it is claimed that there was a *de facto* change, and that the law was framed to protect the people from actual changes. Without deciding how far there may be a *de facto* change, which is not a *de jure* change. I am quite clear in this case, there was no such mandatory and general change as would justify any one in claiming that a change in text-books had been made. Again it is claimed by the respondents, and I think justly, that the substitution of one edition of the same book for another edition, even if the second is fuller and in many respects better than the first, is not a change as contemplated by the law. In such cases the two books are not different books, but different forms of the same book. The only case where such a claim could be maintained, would be where the book had been re-written and made so entirely unlike the old one that the two could not be used together.

Second. I am of the opinion that the notice given January 9th was a legal notice. The law requires that a "notice of the proposed change" shall be given in writing at "a previous regular meeting." The notice in question was given in writing by a member of the committee and constitutes a part of the record of the meeting of January 9th, which was a regular meeting of the committee, so that there can be no question either as to the fact of its having been in writing, or as to the time when it was given.

As to the character of the notice I do not think that the words "proposed change" cover more than the specification of the *kind* of text-book which it is designed to change. The law was obviously passed in the interests of the people, to give the man opportunity to protect themselves from the burdens induced by frequent changes; and the main purpose of this notice was undoubtedly to give the people warning so that they might bring to bear upon the committee, if they saw fit, such influences as would lead them to reconsider their purpose. If such is the fact, it is evident that to the great majority of the people, it would make but little difference what new book was adopted. Moreover the people are not in the position to know of the merits or demerits of different books.

It is also claimed that the notice lacks definiteness because it refers to *some* future meeting. But the law says that the notice must be given at *a* previous regular meeting, which certainly allows some latitude. It could not have been intended that it must have been given at the *preceding* regular meeting, for in that case the law would have used that word, so that I see no deficiency in this particular.

Third. I am of the opinion that the meeting of February 11th was clothed with the power to consider the question of making a change of text-books in geography, because the fact that the law does *not* specify that the changes shall be made at a *regular* meeting, while it does so specify with regard to the "notice," is conclusive evidence that it was not intended to apply the same restriction in both cases. Moreover one can readily see why there is more reason for requiring the notice to be given at a regular meeting, than that the action thereon should be taken at such a meeting. The times of the regular meetings of the committee are generally known and the meetings more or less well attended, or may be, so that the people are thus placed in position to know what is proposed, and to attend to their interests.

If at such a meeting any change is proposed which seems to be objectionable, opportunity is at once afforded for such action as may be deemed best, unless the special meeting were called at a very early day, in which case an appeal would lie on the ground that the action of the committee was a practical nullification of the law. In this case nearly five weeks elapsed between the notice and the action and moreover the subject was considered at a meeting held a week previous, when quite a number of citizens were present, so that it cannot be said that the matter was not known.

In view, therefore, of the above, I do hereby confirm and establish the vote of the school committee of Cranston, passed on the 11th day of February, whereby they adopted Harper & Bros'. geographies for use in the public schools of said town.

T. B. STOCKWELL, C. P. S.

1882.

Approved. C. MATTESON, A. J. S. C.

See Decision No. 5 Page 75.
See Decision No. 13 Page 81.
See Decision No. 23 Page 90.
See Decision No. 47 Page 116.
See Decision No. 71 Page 153.

TEACHERS.

DECISION No. 71.

Case of Layton E. Seamans vs. School Committee of Coventry.

1. Committee have a legal right to refuse to examine a teacher as to literary qualifications if they are dissatisfied with his moral character.
2. A teacher having a county certificate countersigned may be dismissed by school committee for cause.
3. A teacher, having been dismissed, cannot draw teachers' money.

Layton E. Seamans applied to the school committee of Coventry for examination as a teacher of a public school. The committee, however, as they had a legal right, and as they thought upon their oaths they were bound to do, refused to examine him as to his literary qualifications, on the ground that they considered his moral qualifications insufficient for the requirements of the law. Mr. Seamans then succeeded in obtaining a county certificate from John H. Willard, Esq., a county inspector in Providence county, and also obtained the counter signature of the commissioner of public schools; both of these gentlemen supposing that no objections had ever been made to Seamans' moral character. With this certificate thus countersigned, Mr. Seamans entered the school in district No. 5, Coventry, as a teacher. He gave no notice of beginning to the school committee, neither did he in any way conform, or show a disposition to conform, to the rules of the said committee for the government or instruction of the schools of their town.

On the 26th of January, 1855, the committee formally dismissed him from his school, on account, as they alleged, of his having fraudulently procured the above-named county certificate, and non-compliance with their regulations.

Mr. Seamans, however, continued his school to the close of his term, when the school committee granted him an order for the money to pay his wages for the time previous to January 26th, 1855, and refused to grant an order for the time subsequent. It was from this refusal that the appeal was taken.

The commissioner is of opinion that the vote of the school committee, by which Mr. Seamans was dismissed, was a legal and proper vote, and in accordance with the 56th section of the act relating to public schools, which gives to a school committee the power to dismiss a teacher, by whomsoever examined, for just cause. The cause which they alleged appears to be a just and sufficient one. They had after this dismissal no right, according to the 21st section of the act above referred to, to grant any order to Mr. Seamans for services performed as a school teacher in any of the schools of the town, subsequent to the time when he was informed of the act of the school committee by which he was dismissed. The vote of the school committee is therefore affirmed.

R. Allyn, C. P. S.

1855.

DECISION No. 72.

Case of Emor Smith vs. School Committee of Smithfield.

1. The act of one member of a committee, not the act of the committee.
2. Notice to a teacher that he is on trial, is sufficient to proceed with annulment, after the trial.
3. Possession of a certificate entitles teacher to a trial before annulling.
4. Failure to properly instruct and govern, good cause for annulling.

In this case a certificate was legally issued to the appellant and subsequently the clerk of the committee visited his school and not being satisfied therewith immediately sent a note to the trustee that he had annulled the certificate, but sent no notice to the teacher. Another teacher, however, was hired by the trustee. Smith appealed to the commissioner of public schools, and a partial hearing took place on the 27th of January; and on the 31st, the committee failing to appear, the act of Holmes was decided to be void, since in fact no annulment had been made, nothing but a notice having been sent to the trustee that such annulment was made.

The school committee of Smithfield, however, met on the 29th of January, and by a unanimous vote proceeded to annul the certificate of said Smith, given him by Harvey Holmes and dated December 16, 1854, "for deficiency and want of qualification." It is from this vote that the appeal is taken, and in reference to this that the following decisions are made.

The first point made by the appellant was that the decision reversing the act of Holmes, made on the 31st of January, was necessarily conclusive in this, and reversed it also. That, however, was clearly an illegal act done by a single member of the committee, to whom no such power to annul was ever delegated,—in fact, there is no evidence to show that Holmes ever wrote an annulment. He undoubtedly supposed that he had annulled the certificate of Smith, but the contrary is clear; and therefore the committee were at liberty to take original action in the case. It is their act that is to be examined on its own merits. And this can only be justified where it is shown that the circumstances of the case actually called for this course on their part.

A second point made for the appellant was, that he had no notice of the intention of the committee to annul his certificate, and therefore he had no opportunity for trial and defence. It is believed on this point, that the conversation which passed between him and the examiner was notification enough that he was to have four weeks for trial and practical demonstration of his ability to teach and to govern in the school-room. And this is a better form and mode of trial than can be had elsewhere. It is therefore decided that such a trial is sufficient, especially as the teacher always has an appeal, where it can be examined whether the trial in the school was fair and sufficient.

The points made by the committee were two:

1. That Smith was not qualified in literary attainments for the office of teacher.

2. That he failed to comply with the regulations for the schools of Smithfield made by the school committee, and that he failed to impart instruction and to govern his school in a proper manner.

On the first of these points, the commissioner does not feel bound to go back of the certificate of the committee. They, or their clerk, gave him a certificate in proper form, under their oath, after due examination and consideration of the circumstances. It must therefore be held that he was qualified, at least, to make trial of his skill in the school-room.

The case then must turn wholly on the questions, whether or not Smith did comply with the regulations of the school committee, and whether he did really properly instruct and govern his school. The testimony on this point was large in amount and conflicting in character.

·From the facts in the case, as they appear to the commissioner of public schools, it seems to him that the school committee of Smithfield only discharged the duty imposed upon them by the law and by their oath of office, and their act of annulling the certificate of the said Smith ought to be sustained.

R. Allyn, C. P. S.

1855.

Approved. W. R. Staples, C. J. S. C.

DECISION No. 73.

A teacher cannot be required to make fires in a school-room.

R. Allyn, C. P. S.

1855.

See Decision No. 46 Page 112.
See Decision No. 47 Page 116.
See Decision No. 52 Page 123.
See Decision No. 56 Page 125.
See Decision No. 57 Page 126.
See Decision No. 58 Page 128.

LEGAL PROCEEDINGS.

DECISION No. 74.

School commissioner has power to define the bounds of a district, when appealed to from vote of committee.

H. BARNARD, C. P. S.

1848.

Approved. E. R. POTTER, C. P. S.
1852.

Approved. J. B. CHAPIN, C. P. S.
1864.

DECISION No. 75.

School District No. 7, Burrillville.

I am of opinion that the decision of the committee, though not involving the merits of the question, is such as may be appealed from, and that on such appeal the whole merits of the case may be examined and decided.

E. R. POTTER, C. P. S.

1850.

Approved. L. HAILE, A. J. S. C.

DECISION No. 76.

Upon the refusal of the committee, the commissioner may fix the district boundary.

E. R. Potter, C. P. S.

1851.

DECISION No. 77.

School District No. 3, North Providence.

Where express power is not conferred on commissioner, he can, on appeal, simply remand the matter with his decision, and if the official interested will not acquiesce, the remedy is a mandamus from the Supreme Court.

The difficulty which the court experiences in this case results from the 21st section of "the act to revise and amend the law regulating public schools," which defines the duties of the town committee. This section provides that the town committee shall draw orders upon the treasurer for the payment of money due, in conformity with the law: *Provided*, "that the committee shall not be obliged to give any order until they are satisfied the services have actually been performed for which the money is to be paid." They are to decide when money is due, and, having so decided, to draw an order for its payment. And the 23d section of the same act prescribes that "the town treasurer shall receive the money due from the State treasury, and shall keep a separate account of all money appropriated by the State, or town, or otherwise, for public schools, and *shall pay the same to the order of the school committee.*" These two sections are exceedingly significant. The first prescribes who shall draw the orders, and the other what orders the town treasurer shall be bound to pay. The 65th section of the school act gives an appeal from the decision of the school committee to the commissioner, whose decision is to be final. But the commissioner, by this section, has only authority to affirm or reverse the decisions of the town committee, but has no authority to draw orders; and any orders drawn by him are not obligatory upon the town treasurer. We think the proper course for him is to adjudicate upon the appeal, and certify his decision to the town committee, requesting them to draw the order required, and, if they refuse, a mandamus may be granted to compel them to draw the order.

R. W. Greene, C. J. S. C.

1852.

DECISION No. 78.

School District No. 3, North Providence.

I am of opinion that the commissioner has a right to allow a rehearing for good cause, in his discretion; but it is not in the power of the commissioner to dispense with the teacher's having a legal certificate.

E. R. Potter, C. P. S.

1852.

Approved. R. W. Greene, C. J. S. C.

DECISION No. 79.

Transfer of land does not make another appraisal of a lot necessary, and the failure from sickness to make an appeal invalidates the claim to make another, without special legislation.

J. KINGSBURY, C. P. S.

1856.

Approved. E. R. POTTER, A. J. S. C.

DECISION No. 80.

Petition of Emor Smith for Rehearing.

1. Rehearing not possible after approval by a judge of the Supreme Court.
2. Commissioner to make up a statement of facts from the evidence, but not to submit the evidence as such to the judge.
3. Jurisdiction of the commissioner.

In the matter of the decision of the commissioner of public schools in case of the appeal of Emor Smith from a vote of the school committee of Smithfield, annulling the certificate of said Smith as a teacher in said town.

This is a motion or petition for a reconsideration, by the commissioner and the judge, of the above decision, on the ground that the decision of the commissioner reported to the Hon. William R. Staples, late Chief Justice of the Supreme Court, on the 24th day of August, 1855, and approved on the 26th day of September, 1855, is not valid and binding, because the commissioner did not report a statement of the facts as they were sworn to or admitted, but instead thereof reported *as facts* his own conclusions upon the testimony; it appearing from the petition of said Smith that "he insists that there can be no final or binding decision, until a *statement of the evidence* shall be made to the judge," for reasons by him in his petition set forth.

The 65th section of the "act to revise and amend the laws regulating public schools," provides "that the commissioner may (and if requested on the hearing of either party shall) lay a statement of the facts of the case before some one of the judges of the Supreme Court, whose approval of such decision shall be final." If then, in the matter of this decision, upon such request, a statement of the facts of this case, in the sense of the statute, has been laid before one of the judges of the Supreme Court, and the decision of the commissioner has been by him approved, this "approval" is, by the very words of the statute, made final, irrespective of the merits of the decision approved. The "appeal" in other words, in the civil law sense of the term, and as it is used in our statutes,—that is, a rehearing of the whole cause, matter of fact as well as law, after it has been decided by a competent tribunal,—is expressly given, by the first words of the section of the school act above referred to, to the commissioner; and the section provides that his decision upon such appeal shall be final, if the commissioner, upon the request of either party, shall "lay a statement of the facts of the case" before one of the judges of the Supreme Court, and he shall approve the decision. The purpose of this last provision was, undoubtedly, to give to the commissioner and the parties the aid of such a judicial officer in matters of law, and to secure, as far as conveniently practicable, by an uniform construction of the act, an uniform system of legislation upon so important and interesting a subject as the discipline and government of our public schools.

The document entitled "Decision of commissioner of public schools in case of appeal of E. Smith from a vote of the school committee of Smithfield annulling the certificate of Smith as teacher in said town," signed by Robert Allyn, commissioner of public schools, is, in my judgment, "*a statement of facts*" by the commissioner in the sense of the 65th section of the school act, although it is not, as it is averred by the petitioner that it is not, a statement of the testimony or evidence by means of which the commissioner ascertained the facts which he states in it. "A statement of facts" from testimony or evidence must from its very nature, be the conclusions of the officer entitled to make it, from the testimony or evidence which he has heard; and the distinction between such a statement, and a statement of the evidence or testimony upon which it is based, is too well settled in legal practice and parlance to require illustration. Whether the conclusions drawn from the evidence or testimony by the commissioner were legitimate or not, is a matter which the law does not, in my judgment, confide to the judge, but solely to the commissioner, who alone hears the appeal, listens to the witnesses, examines the evidence, and arrives at the conclusion of what are "*the facts of the case.*" No power, no means, are, in my judgment, given to the judge to examine into these facts. It is the duty of the commissioner, under the law, to decide what the facts are, and to lay a statement of them before the judge, with his decision upon them, and the sole office and jurisdiction of the judge is, upon such statement, to approve or disapprove the decision of the commissioner. This is not only plain from the words of the act, but is to be inferred from the nature of the facts to be ascertained,—the good or ill discipline of schools, the fitness or unfitness of teachers to instruct or discipline scholars, and the like facts, peculiarly fitted to be ascertained from evidence by the commissioner, but which the judge would ordinarily have no such peculiar qualifications to ascertain.

The jurisdiction of the school commissioner under the public school act, by way of appeal from the decisions or doings of school committees, district meetings, trustees and county inspectors, is, looking to the subject, nature and manner of its exercise, rather a visitatorial power, than that of an ordinary legal tribunal, and the power of the judge of the Supreme Court in the matter of such an appeal is limited, precisely as might have been anticipated from the universal course in such cases, to the mere approval of the decision of the commissioner upon his statement of the facts.

It being admitted by the petitioner in his said petition that the decision and statement of facts of the commissioner in the matter of this appeal was laid by the commissioner before Chief Justice Staples on the 24th of August, 1855, and that the said decision was, by said Chief Justice Staples, then one of the judges of the Supreme Court, approved,—and it appearing to me that the statement of facts submitted to said judge, was such a statement of facts as is required by the statutes, and that his approval thereupon of the decision of the commissioner is final,—I therefore approve the decision of the commissioner that this motion or petition for reconsideration must be by him dismissed for want of any jurisdiction in him alone or in him conjointly with a judge of the Supreme Court, to rehear or reconsider the decision so approved.

After such a decision and approval made, neither the commissioner nor Judge Staples, if the latter were still in office, could rehear or reconsider the matter of the same, no matter how erroneous such decision and approval might be. Much less can the commissioner, with another judge of the Supreme Court, or subject to approval of such judge, whether then in office or succeeding to the office of Judge Staples, reconsider and rejudge his approval.

S. Ames, C. J. S. C.

1856.

DECISION No. 81.

School District No. 10, North Providence.

The school commissioner has no jurisdiction in an appeal from a vote of a school district to enforce a claim against the collector of a district.

The appellant, tax collector of school district No. 10, North Providence, has suffered no grievance at the hands of the district, of which he can complain to the school commissioner. He has collected money which the district demands of him, as they have the right. His answer is. that he has paid it to the treasurer; but as the treasurer denies this, and the evidence of payment produced by the collector is not satisfactory, the district very properly persist in their demand. The appellant's admission charges him with the money, and he produces no sufficient evidence, as it would seem, in his discharge. A mere demand of money as due, though unfounded, is no ground of legal complaint, and this demand, under the circumstances was natural and proper.

Besides a money claim of this sort, made by a school district against its collector or treasurer, seems to be wholly without the jurisdiction of the commissioner. He can issue no execution to enforce it, nor can he enjoin any suit commenced upon it. It must necessarily be adjusted by the ordinary tribunals of the law, which are clothed with powers to aid the right, in the way both of pursuit and defence. The school law, by enabling school districts to require bonds of their clerks, collectors and treasurers, points to the ordinary legal remedies against such officers in case they do not faithfully account for moneys received by them, or damages are sought against them for other breach of official duty.

The school commissioner in my judgment was right in dismissing this appeal.

S. Ames, C. J. S. C.

1861.

DECISION No. 82.

School District No. 7, North Providence.

An award of appraisers is void, unless both the owner of the land and the representative of the district are heard at one and the same hearing.

In a suit against a school district, on an award of appraisers of the value of a lot taken for a school-house under Ch. 66, as amended by Ch. 323, of the Revised Statutes, it appearing, that at the meeting of the district clerk and of the plaintiff, upon notice, before the appraisers for hearing upon the matter of the valuation of the lot, the plaintiff, when going with the appraisers upon the land, with coarse and violent language forbade the clerk to accompany them, who thereupon remained behind, and the plaintiff in the absence of the clerk was heard by the appraisers; *it was held*, that the award thus made by the appraisers was void, and could confer no right of action in favor of the plaintiff against the district.

It was the right of the defendants to be present at all times during the hearing, that they might know and hear whatever was offered to the referees, either by way of evidence or argument, by the plaintiff; that they might know what was necessary to be answered by proof or by argument, and, especially, that they might see that no improper communication was made, or illegal evidence offered, to the referees. . . . .

We are of the opinion that the award obtained should be held void.

S. Ames, C. J. S. C.

1863.

DECISION No. 83.

School District No. 19, South Kingstown.

Appeals may be made from decisions of committees in locating school-houses.

Objection is made to the decision of the commissioner in this case, that it is not a case where the law gives any right of appeal, and that therefore the decision of the school committee was final and conclusive, as was decided in the case of John H. Gardner, reported in 4 R. I., 602.

The grounds of the argument against the right of appeal in this case, could not, of course, be more ably stated than they are in the decision to which the counsel refers us.

And they are, First. That a grievance implies a wrong growing out of some infraction of law; a litigated question of right. The present case involves no question of violated right and therefore the appellant is not a party aggrieved. Second. That the discretion is with the school committee; they have the power to decide it, and no wrong is done to any one, and no one has a right to complain, or correct them. Third. That a contrary construction would throw every discretionary power into the hands of the commissioner and the Supreme Court, which latter might be utterly unfit to exercise it.

First. Is the appellant a party aggrieved? He is a property holder in the district. The owners of that property have or may have children entitled to the privileges of the school. The distance of the location from his dwelling may seriously affect, not only the convenience of sending to school, but the value of his property hereafter. If the money was a gift from some one to found a school, he might dictate the site and the conditions of his bounty, and no one could legally complain. Here the whole money, as well what comes from the State and town treasuries to pay the teacher, as the money to build the house, is derived from taxation, of which the appellant, it is presumed, pays his fair proportion. Some hundreds of years ago, perhaps, a deprivation of school privileges might not be considered a grievance; hardly so now. The appellant pays his proportion of the whole expenditure, and has a very material interest in the proper application of it.

Second. Does the fact that the school committee exercise a discretion in the choice of a site, prevent an appeal?

To apply such a doctrine to the school law would almost nullify the provisions for appeal.

There is hardly an exercise of power by the school committee or trustees which does not imply the exercise of discretion. The mere giving an order for payment of wages may, perhaps, be an exception; but the examining, and, in some cases, employing teachers, annulling of certificates, forming and changing school districts, supervision of taxes and building of houses, and the general regulation of the schools, all imply discretion. So with trustees; and so, in many cases, with the powers vested in school districts. If, because they have the power to decide in the first place, and because they exercise a discretion in doing it, there can be no appeal, there would be hardly a case left for the exercise of such a right.

And yet the language of the provision is very broad, and it would seem difficult, without a great deal of verbiage, to make it more comprehensive.

If there was any doubt as to the meaning of the law, there is another principle of decision which might be resorted to for aid. When a law admits of different constructions, it is well settled that the usage un-

15

der it, and the practical construction of it for a series of years, is entitled to great weight, and sometimes may be decisive.

In the present case the practice was uniform. The first two commissioners under the law were constantly engaged in examining appeals of this very sort, sometimes confirming and sometimes altering, or wholly revising, decisions of committees as to sites of school-houses. The re-districting, which the law rendered necessary in most of the towns, led to frequent dissension. And the practice was continued under their successors, and does not seem to have even been questioned until 1858.

It would no doubt make the office of commissioner easier and more pleasant, to take away this power. The decision of such cases leads frequently to enmities, or charges of being subject to improper influence.

School committees, however honest, may be subject to local influence; and the very knowledge that their determination was likely to be reviewed by a disinterested person, might, in many cases, prevent an improper decision. And a commissioner would seldom revise a decision of a committee, unless he was satisfied that the public good or justice to individuals required it.

And, for the purpose of securing uniformity in the administration of the law, this provision is very important.

Third. The third objection is that the allowance of appeals would refer everything to the discretion of the commissioner and judge,—the latter, probably, not much acquainted with the subject, and unfitted for the exercise of this power.

It was deemed essential to the success of a comparatively new system to prevent litigation, if possible. A quarrel or a lawsuit in a school-district is generally not long confined to the original parties. It spreads among all the families; it goes into the selection of teachers, and impairs the discipline of the schools; and, if the difficulty once takes the shape of a lawsuit, and the parties have expended money as well as temper upon it, it is still more difficult to settle. Hence the provision for a cheap and speedy decision, avoiding the delay and expense of a lawsuit, and as the commissioner would, probably, very often not be a lawyer, it was provided that he might resort to a judge for an opinion upon points of law.

The practical construction of the law from the beginning has been that the judge has nothing to do with deciding the facts in the case. (See "School Law," edition of 1857, remarks page 55; and see, also, decision of Judge Ames, in case of Emor Smith. R. I. Reports, vol. iv., 590, 592, 594.) The judge would not reverse the decision of a commissioner, unless there appeared to be a legal objection to its validity.

Being therefore of opinion that the commissioner had jurisdiction on appeal, I see no reason for reversing his decision; but as, until confirmed, the commissioner might rehear if he deems it expedient, and after confirmation the decision would be final, and could not be reheard by him, and the location could not be changed without beginning proceedings again before the committee, I postpone a formal confirmation.

E. R. Potter, A. J. S. C.

1873.

DECISION No. 84.

In towns where the district system prevails, neither town nor town treasurer is liable for teacher's wages, at least until an order has been given therefor by the school committee.

This case was submitted to the Supreme Court for Kent county on the following agreed statement of facts:

"1. School District No. 17, of the town of Warwick, is indebted to the plaintiff in the sum of $125; due to said plaintiff as a teacher of the public school in said district.

"2. On or about the day of , A. D. 1876, suit was begun against the plaintiff in the Justice Court of the town of Warwick, by one Oliver P. Matteson, upon a writ of attachment, which directed, among other things, that the officer should trustee or attach moneys in the hands and possession of the town of Warwick due said plaintiff.

"3. That said attachment was intended to reach the moneys earned by said plaintiff as teacher in the school district No. 17, he being employed by the trustees of said district as teacher, in said town, and that a copy of said writ was served upon the town treasurer of said town for that purpose, there being no command in said writ to serve, nor was any copy in fact served, upon any officer of said district No. 17.

"4. That there were no moneys due from said town of Warwick to the plaintiff, nor any moneys of his in the hands of said town either directly or indirectly, except such as were supposed to go to said plaintiff for his services as teacher of the public school in said district.

"5. Said Matteson obtained final judgment against said plaintiff in the suit commenced in the Justice Court as aforesaid.

"6. There was no debt or demand of any kind laid by the plaintiff against said town other than the supposed claim mentioned in section 4 above.

"7. It is hereby agreed that jury trial be waived."

(East Greenwich, March 17, 1877. *Per Curiam.*)

The statute provides that moneys appropriated to, and raised by, the several towns for schools shall be kept by their respective treasurers, subject to the order of their respective school committees. Gen. Stat. R. I. cap. 47, § 6. A school committee may give its order either in favor of the trustees or treasurer of a school district, or directly in favor of a teacher. Cap. 53, § 17. Teachers, where towns are districted, are employed by the trustees of the districts; Cap. 52, § 1; and neither town nor town treasurer is made liable for their wages otherwise than upon the order of the school committee. We think, therefore, that where a town is districted neither town nor town treasurer is liable to garnishment in respect of any teachers' wages, until at least an order has been given in favor of such teacher by the school committee of the town. This does not appear to have been done in the case at bar. The judgment, agreeably to the agreement, must be for the plaintiff for the full amount of his claim.

DECISION No. 85.

Where a school committee decline to act, in cases where such action is discretionary with them, no appeal can be taken to the commissioner.

T. B. Stockwell, C. P. S.

1882.

Approved. C. Matteson, A. J. S. C.

REMARKS.

BOARD OF EDUCATION.

In addition to the general supervision and control of the schools of the State, which the statutes confer on the Board of Education, the following specific duties are devolved upon them :—The election of the commissioner of public schools; the care and oversight of the free public libraries and distribution of the annual State appropriation therefor; the apportionment of the appropriation for evening schools, and the supervision of their work; the management and control of the State School for the Deaf; the decision of all cases of remission of fines, penalties and forfeiture arising under the school laws, and the presentation of an annual report to the General Assembly. The Board of Education, together with the commissioner of public schools, constitute the Trustees of the State Normal school and are vested with the entire control and management of the same, subject, in the matter of expenditures, to the amount appropriated for the school by the General Assembly. The regular meetings of the Board occur quarterly on the first Thursday of the months of March, June, September and December.

THE COMMISSIONER OF PUBLIC SCHOOLS.

The commissioner is secretary of the Board of Education, and its executive officer in the administration of the school system of the State. His duties are to advise with school officers, teachers and others, in all matters relating to education; to visit and inspect the schools of the State as often as practicable; to deliver addresses in the several towns on subjects relating to the progress of the schools; to arrange and conduct teachers' institutes in various parts of the State, as the various localities may demand; to recommend and secure, as far as is desirable, a local uniformity of text-books; to assist in the establishment of, and selection of books for, school libraries; to apportion the State appropriations for day schools and school apparatus; to collect and collate the statistics relating to public schools, and to present an annual report to the Board of Education upon the state of the schools, with plans and suggestions for their improvement.

The commissioner is also a judicial adviser on all questions arising under the administration of the school laws, and is required to hear and decide all cases presented by appeal or otherwise, free of expense to the parties. In the words of the late Chief Justice Ames, the commissioner is "in legal idea, the visitor of the public schools of the State—a domestic judge—whose short and noiseless method of settling disputes arising between the different officers and members of this academic body is intended to preserve that peace and harmony which are so essential to its well-being."

TOWNS.

In each town the schools are carried on under the town or the district system. Where the former prevails, the schools are wholly in charge of the school committee of the town, subject in all cases to the supervision of the commissioner of public schools. Under the district system, the trustee has the superintendence of the school property of the district, and contracts with teachers, while the school committee exercise all other authority over the schools.

The simplicity, unity and economy of the town system are in favor of its universal adoption, and any town may, by a vote at the annual town meeting, so far relinquish the district system, as to place the entire management of the schools in the hands of the school committee of the town, notice of the proposed change having been inserted in the warrant for the town meeting; but the school property will still remain in the control of the districts.

Each town is required to maintain a system of schools, and to appropriate for their maintenance a sum at least equal to that received from the State, under the provision of chapter 49. Any town which shall fail or refuse to raise for schools the above sum forfeits its proportion of the State appropriation, for the benefit of the school fund of the State, but is not relieved from its obligation to maintain schools.

Towns are authorized to establish and maintain free public libraries and are permitted to assess a tax, not exceeding twenty-five cents on each hundred dollars of ratable property, for the founding of such libraries, and an annual tax, not exceeding twenty cents on each one thousand dollars of ratable property, for the support and increase thereof.

TOWN CLERKS.

It is the duty of the several town clerks, or of some person appointed by the town council, to take the school census annually and make return thereof, as required by law, to the school committee; they are also to distribute to the persons designated, all such school blanks and other documents as may be sent to them. In those cases where the town is divided into districts the town clerk is required to keep a record of the district boundaries and of all changes therein; and he should provide a special book for that purpose.

TOWN TREASURERS.

The town treasurer, as soon as the town has voted the annual appropriation for public schools, or before the first of July in each year, should make his return to the commissioner as required by law. This return must contain a statement of the amount expended by the town for school purposes, and the sources from which it was derived; and also a statement of the amount appropriated for public schools for the next year. Failure to make such return will prevent the payment of the town's share of the public money.

He is to keep a separate account of all school moneys, and is, before the first day of July in each year, to furnish the school committee with a particular account of all moneys applicable to the support of public schools for the current school year, specifying the sources of the same. He can only pay out the school money, whether derived from the State, town, or registry tax, upon orders signed by the chairman or clerk of the school committee, and if he should pay it out or appropriate it otherwise, he would be liable to the penalty of the law.

Special attention is now called to the fact that the law requires that the amount of money received from registry taxes shall be kept out of the school fund till the first Monday in May of each year, when the whole amount received during the year is to be credited to the school account. It is desirable that this provision of the law, as also a similar one in reference to the dog taxes, should be strictly obeyed, as it will aid very much in securing correct reports each year.

It is very desirable that the town treasurer's returns to the commissioner should be made, as the law requires, on or before July 1st, because failure to do so is very vexatious, and will delay, if not stop, the payment of the town's share of the State money. It is also very necessary that the returns of the treasurer shall cover the same period of time as that covered by the returns of the school committee. The object of the law requiring returns from each source is that they may be used to verify each other and thus secure freedom from mistakes. But this cannot be done if they are made out for different periods of time.

SCHOOL COMMITTEES.

Great care should be taken by the several towns in the selection and election of the best *men and women* to this office. No political issues should hinder the election of competent persons to this most responsible office of the town. The interests of the children are too valuable to be entrusted to those who know not and care not with reference to their future welfare.

The law allows competent women, as well as men, to be elected to this office, and experience shows that women have most faithfully, conscientiously and successfully fulfilled its duties. Their time, interest, sympathies, and benevolent purposes eminently qualify them for the duties, and a portion of each school board may well be constituted of active and efficient women. The one condition imposed by law upon membership is residence in the town. The one disqualification is a pecuniary interest in any school text-book.

It is believed that in all cases it will be better to have the town's committee a small rather than a large one. Their duties are to examine teachers, visit, and have a supervision of the schools. There is danger that a large committee will not meet often, and that they will attempt to perform too many of their duties by small sub-committees of one or more. The delegation, by the whole committee to each member, of the power to manage some particular district has always been a great cause of the inefficiency of our system. The whole committee should have some knowledge of *all* of the schools, and the persons appointed to visit particular schools should always make specific reports to the whole board at their monthly or quarterly sessions. In this way alone can the annual report of the school committee be made up properly and as fully as is necessary. Special attention to the duties of examination of schools alone can fit the committee to make such annual communication to the people of the town on the subject of their schools as shall be of the greatest service to them. *This annual report should by all means be printed and circulated among all the citizens of the town, as the law provides.* The mothers and the sisters of the scholars should see it as well as the fathers and voters, and the only way in which they can all enjoy this privilege is to have it printed, and at least one copy furnished to each family in the town. It is then easy to make all citizens acquainted with the workings of our school system, and to induce them, both to make ample provisions for its support and to guard carefully the expenditures made for the common benefit.

At the first meeting of the committee after the annual town meeting, they should organize by the election of a chairman and clerk, who are removable by the committee only for cause and after a hearing. It would be well to have the certificate of the election and engagement of the several members of the committee made upon the record book itself, as loose papers are more liable to be lost.

The number of the school committee in each town is now fixed by statute law at the number constituting the committee on the first day of February, 1882, and cannot be changed except by special act of the General Assembly. If the town fails to elect the requisite number at the annual town meeting, the town council must elect them at its *next* meeting. Any town may vote to delegate to the council the entire power of appointing the committee.

Vacancies.—If any member of the committee resigns, removes or dies, the vacancy must be supplied by the town council until the next town meeting, which then fills the vacancy for the unexpired term, or refers it to the council, which proceeds to do the same.

Meetings.—They must hold four meetings in each year at least. The times for these regular meetings should be fixed by a by-law of the committee, in order that people having business to do before the committee may know when to attend. But as a general rule the schools cannot prosper unless meetings are held as often as once a month. By frequent meetings and conversation much valuable information may be acquired. And it would be well for committees to be continually endeavoring to obtain a knowledge of the situation of the different districts, the amount of taxable property in each district, the number and character of the different classes of population respectively, etc., and this sort of information should be preserved, as it is absolutely necessary to enable them and their successors to discharge well their duties.

All acts of the school committee, to be valid, must be done at a *meeting* of the committee. Giving their assent to any measure separately, and without meeting, would be held illegal.

The manner of calling special meetings of the committee should be regulated by by-law. If there be no by-law, the chairman or clerk should call them, and should give every member notice.

Before the first day of July in each year, the school committee are entitled to receive from the town treasurer a report of all school moneys in his hands, or to be received, which will be applicable for the support of public schools for the current school year, specifying particularly the sources whence derived.

Laying off Districts.—In towns divided into districts, the whole power of making new districts, altering old ones, and of settling disputed boundaries, is vested by law in the school committee, subject to an appeal to the commissioner. Notice must be given in all cases by posting on the school-houses and sending to the trustees, of the districts liable to be affected, notice of the meeting and of the proposed changes, for at least five days, previous thereto.

In laying off districts, regard should be had to the convenience of attending school, the number of scholars, the valuation of property, and ability to provide school-houses, etc. It will be always expedient to bound them by rivers, roads, or other natural or well-known boundaries, when practicable. When the lines can, without inconvenience, be so drawn as to include all of any person's farm in the same district where his dwelling-house is, it will save a great deal of trouble and expense in assessing taxes, but in all cases the lines should be continuous.

Districts must be set off by bounds including certain land. It is not sufficient to declare that a district shall be composed of such and such *persons*. The Supreme Court of Massachusetts has declared such districts to be invalid. [7 Pick. 106, and 12 Pick. 206.]

When a district which has built a school-house is divided, or its bounds altered so as to take off any portion of it, the joint property is to be equitably apportioned among the several parts. If the district owes any debts, they should of course be considered in the apportionment. In some cases this can be done by a division of the property itself. In other cases the rent or income may be apportioned, according to the peculiar circumstances. The school committee must decide such cases, subject, of course, to the appeal provided by the law.

Where it is much more convenient for a person belonging to one district or town to send to a school in another district or town the policy of both school committees and trustees should be to extend the advantages of the schools as freely as the circumstances will permit. The State is now so large a contributor to the support of the great majority of the schools, that the advantages thereof ought to be made as available as possible. The authority to admit or send from one district to another in the same town is now in the school committee. If the pupils come from outside of the town, the trustees have the authority, subject to the approval of the school committee.

As a rule district lines should not be changed, except for good and sufficient reasons. Frequent changes of boundary lines tend to confusion and error in the assessment of taxes and other business. In every town where the district system prevails it would be well to have a description of the districts *printed* for general information and circulation. This might, with propriety, be attached to the school regulations. The law also provides that the town clerk shall keep a record of the district boundaries and all changes must be reported to him.

The power of forming *joint* districts on the borders of the different towns is also confided to the school committees. Many of the manufacturing villages are on streams which are the boundaries of towns, and are partly in both towns. In such situations the school committees should encourage the union of the adjoining districts, as both together will probably be able to establish a graded school; or at least to maintain a better and a longer school than either one alone.

In assigning to a district or portion thereof, which forms part of a joint district, its proportion of that part of the money which is divided according to average attendance, the committee will of course take the average attendance of that portion of the scholars who belong to their own town.

Location, Plans, etc.—The school committee are to locate all school-houses, and to approve of all plans and specifications for building or repairing them, and all district taxes for whatever purpose. When the district is unanimous, and the location on the whole unobjectionable, the committee should defer to their wishes; but in cases of dispute, they should endeavor to select such a site as will best accommodate the greater portion of the district, and at the same time fulfill the conditions of a good site. In this connection it should be said that the size of the school-house lot is of great importance and the committee may not unlikely find it necessary sometimes to condemn a location on account of its unsuitable size. If a district is unable to secure by purchase a lot acceptable to the committee, the committee are authorized to proceed and select a lot and appoint three disinterested persons to appraise its value, and upon tender of said sum to the owner of the land the title is vested in the district. If the owner is aggrieved he may appeal to the next common pleas court for the county in which the district is located, by giving bond to prosecute his appeal and by producing an attested copy of the whole proceedings to such court, and filing his reasons of appeal with the clerk of the court ten days before the sitting thereof. Such appeal opens the whole case, both as to the necessity of taking the land, and the valuation thereof.

The provision that all taxes which any district may order must be approved by the school committee was intended to operate as a salutary check against the improper exercise of the power given to school districts. In some districts there may be but few legal voters; in others, the majority of voters may be persons not interested in the property in the district; and various other cases may happen where a minority should be protected against abuse of taxation. And for this purpose, the law requires the approbation of the school committee, the majority of whom will probably belong to other parts of the town, and have no private or personal interest in the local controversies and disputes of the district.

For the same and other reasons the law requires the plan of building to be approved by the committee. The committee should therefore investigate this subject, and visit and examine the best school-houses, and consult the best authorities on heating, ventilation, lighting, etc., so as to be prepared to act when called on. Moreover, the committees should not always wait till called upon, before acting in reference to the condition of the school-buildings. The responsibility for seeing that the buildings used for school purposes are suitable rests with the committee, and they should not hesitate to act accordingly.

Examining Teachers.—In towns acting under the district system the examination of persons wishing to teach either as principals or assistants, the granting of certificates of qualification, and the annulling of such certificates, are among the most important duties devolving on the school committee, and on their faithful performance the efficiency of the law largely depends.

The inefficiency of the school system in most of the towns may be traced to the fact that the duties of examining teachers and visiting the schools are too generally neglected or ill-performed.

The law gives the committee the power to appoint a sub-committee for the purpose of examining teachers, or they may impose the duty upon the superintendent. But it is respectfully suggested that where the whole committee can meet for this purpose it is most advisable. It will have a better effect upon the teachers themselves, and incompetent persons will be less likely to present themselves. It is certain that the authority to grant certificates should never be vested by a committee in two bodies or persons at the same time. Such a division of responsibility is always attended with disastrous results. Where the duty of examining and certificating teachers is imposed upon the superintendent or a sub-committee, the action of such subcommittee or superintendent should be final. To allow an appeal to the committee is to weaken the force and value of the authority, opinions and decisions of the examiner.

In making such examinations, whether by the whole board or by the sub-committee, they should inquire:

First, as to moral character. On this point the committee should be entirely satisfied before proceeding further. Some opinion can be formed from the general deportment and language of the applicant; but the safest course will be, with regard to those who are strangers to the committee, to insist on the written testimony of persons of the highest respectability in the towns and neighborhoods where they have resided; and especially to require the certificate of the school committee and parents where they have taught before, as to the character they have sustained, and the influence they have exerted in the school and in society.

While a committee should not endeavor to inquire into the peculiar religious or sectarian opinions of a teacher, and should not entertain any preferences or prejudices founded on any such grounds, they ought, without hesitation to reject every person who is in the habit of ridiculing, deriding or scoffing at religion.

And while an examination should in no case be extended to the *political* opinions of the candidates, yet it may with propriety extend "to their manner in expressing such belief, or maintaining it. If that manner is in itself boisterous and disorderly, intemperate and offensive, it may well be supposed to indicate ungoverned passions, or want of sound principles of conduct, which would render its possessor obnoxious to the inhabitants of the district, and unfit for the sacred duties of a teacher of youth, who should instruct by example as well as by precept."—*N. Y. Regulations.*

Second, as to literary attainments. The lowest grade of attainments demands a thorough knowledge of the common branches of English education. Every teacher should prove, either by examination, or by previous experience, which must have come to the personal knowledge of the committee, his ability to teach the English language, arithmetic, penmanship, geography and history. In an examination as to the attainments of a teacher in these branches it should be so conducted as to test his capacity, in those particulars, to teach any grade of schools. And in granting certificates some reference may be had to the condition and wants of the particular schools for which the candidates are presented. But no person should be considered qualified to teach any school, who cannot speak and write the English language, if not elegantly, at least correctly. He should be a good reader, and be able to make the hearer understand and feel all that the author intended. He should be able to give the analysis, as well as explain the meaning of the words of the sentence, and explain all dates, names and allusions. He should be a good speller; and to test this, as well as his knowledge of punctuation, the use of capitals, etc., he should be required to write out his answers to some of the questions of the committee. He should understand practically the first principles of English grammar, as illustrated in his own writing and conversation. He should be able to write a good hand, and to teach others how to do so. He should show his knowledge of geography by applying his definitions of the elementary principles to the geography of his own town, State and country, and by questions on the map and globe. He should be able to answer promptly all questions relating to the leading events of the history of the United States, and of his own State. In arithmetic, he should be well versed in some treatise on mental arithmetic, and have a clear and definite knowledge of the principles of written arithmetic, and be able to work out before the committee, on the blackboard or slate, such questions as will test his ability to teach accurately and successfully the topics prescribed for the class of schools in which he will be engaged.

In addition to the above qualifications every teacher should possess at least an elementary knowledge of physiology and the laws of health. Such knowledge is indispensable to the proper regulation of the air, temperature and light of the school-room; and also to that care of the children which should be given to them daily if they are to do their best work at school, or are to grow up to lives of vigorous manhood and womanhood. A knowledge also of English literature, sufficient to enable the teacher to give to the selections of the reading-book more attractions and also to guide the pupils in their reading outside of school hours is very desirable and should be insisted upon so far as possible. And in addition to the above, some familiarity with the elements of natural history and free-hand drawing will be found of great advantage both to teacher and school. Of course, for the upper grammar and high schools, the standard of qualifications of the teachers will be set by the course of studies adopted by the committee.

Third, as to ability to instruct. This ability includes aptness to teach, a power of simplifying difficult processes, a skill in imparting knowledge, and of inducing pupils to try, and to try in such a way that they will derive encouragement as they go along; all of which must be given by nature, but may be cultivated by observation and practice. An examination into the literary qualifications of a candidate as ordinarily conducted, and even when conducted by an experienced committee, or even by a teacher, will not always determine whether this ability is possessed, or possessed in a very eminent degree. Hence it is desirable for the committee to ascertain what success the candidate has had in other places, if he has taught before; and if this evidence cannot be had, whether he has received any instruction in the art of teaching; or has been educated under a successful teacher; or has visited good schools. In conducting the examination to ascertain this point, the candidate should be asked how he would teach the several studies. He should be asked how he would proceed in teaching a child to read, who had never been instructed at all; as for example, whether he would give him sentences, words or single letters; and then the methods he would employ, how far he would combine writing with reading, and what use he would make of the blackboard. So in spelling, he should be asked how he would classify his scholars in this branch, and the methods of arranging and conducting a class exercise; how far he would put out the word to the whole class, and after requiring all to spell it *mentally*, name a particular scholar to spell it *orally;* how far he would adopt the method of writing the words, and especially the difficult ones, on a slate or blackboard; how far he would connect spelling with the reading lessons, etc.

It will be more satisfactory sometimes, perhaps, to have a class of small scholars present at the examination, and let the candidate go through an exercise with them, so that the committee can have a practical specimen of his tact in teaching each branch of study, in explaining and removing difficulties, etc.

The same method of examination should be carried into reading, and every other branch. It is more important to know that the teacher has sound views as to methods, than that he is qualified as to literary attainments, for the most extensive knowledge is of little value if one does not possess the ability to use it successfully.

Fourth, ability to govern. This is an important qualification, insisted upon by the law, and indispensable to the success of the schools. On this point the committee should call for the evidence of former experience, wherever the candidate has taught before, and when this cannot be had, the examination should elicit the plans of the teacher as to making children comfortable, keeping them all usefully employed, and interested in their studies, his best system of rewards and punishments, and examples of the kinds of punishment he would resort to in particular cases, and all other information pertaining to the good order and government of a school. In this connection, the age, manners, bearing, knowledge of the world, love and knowledge of children, etc., of the applicant, will deserve attention.

In addition to these qualifications which the law requires, the address and personal manners and habits of the applicant should be inquired into, for these will determine, in a great measure, the manners and habits of the children whom he will be called upon to teach.

The most thorough and satisfactory mode of conducting the literary examination is by written questions and answers; if the examination is conducted orally, it will be desirable to keep minutes of the questions and answers.

The school committee must remember that on the thoroughness and fidelity with which this duty is performed depends, in a great measure, the success or failure of the school system. The whole machinery moves to bring good teachers into the schools, and to keep them as long, and under as favorable circumstances, as possible.

If the teacher adds to his other qualifications a knowledge of the art of singing, it will be an additional recommendation of him with those who desire to have a good school. Singing in school serves as a recreation and an amusement, especially for the smaller scholars. It exercises and strengthens their voices and lungs, and, by its influence on the disposition and morals, enables a teacher to govern his school with comparative ease.

The committee should exercise a sound discretion in the examination, for the sole responsibility rests upon them in determining who shall, and who shall not, teach in our schools. No appeal can be taken to the commissioner from the refusal of a committee to grant a certificate.

If a person has been before examined by them, and the committee have often visited his school, and know him to be a good teacher, the law allows them to give him a certificate, founded on this experience. But the re-examination can in no case do any injury, and by gradually increasing their rigor and adding to the requirements, much may be done towards raising the general standard of education. The committee should, for convenience of reference, keep a tabular list of the names of all persons examined by them, either on their common record book, or in a book kept for that purpose, with columns for the date, age, place of residence of the applicant, the result of the examination, and any other remarks that may appear worthy of remembrance.

In towns where the whole control of the schools is in the hands of the committee, the law does not require that certificates be issued to the teachers, but it is especially the duty of the committee to see that none but well qualified teachers are employed. In such towns where there is no division of power in the management of the schools, there ought to be the best results.

Annulling certificates and dismissing teachers. As a teacher's qualifications depend not merely upon his learning (of which a committee can judge from examination), but upon his moral character, his disposition and temper, and his capacity to impart information and to govern a school, in regard to all of which the committee may be deceived or not fully informed; the law gives the committee the power to annul any certificate they may have given, if, on trial, the teacher proves unqualified. A teacher may also refuse to adopt the proper books, may introduce improper books, may refuse to adopt what the committee deem the best methods of instruction or discipline, or may violate other regulations of the committee, in which cases the committee have full power to dismiss the teacher. In case of all annulments of certificates of teachers or dismission, the school committee, who are the only authority in the matter, must give at least five days' notice in writing of such intention, and a hearing, and afterwards must notify the trustee of their act.

Visiting schools. There is no duty of the school

committee more generally neglected than that of visiting schools.

The law makes it the *express duty* of committees and trustees to visit the schools often. Without personal visits to the schools, either by themselves or the superintendent, the committee can know nothing about the teacher's capacity to impart information, or about his methods of instruction and government, or the progress of the pupils, neither can they know the state of the register and the general condition of the school.

Visiting the schools also has the effect of encouraging the teacher in the performance of his duties; and if the teacher is visited and treated with proper respect by the committee, trustees and parents, it materially aids to secure to him respectful treatment from the scholars, and enables him to govern his school and preserve order with ease, and without resorting to corporal punishment.

But the greatest influence is on the pupils themselves. School is too apt to be considered by many of them as a place of punishment. But if their parents and others visit them often, and take an interest in their studies and progress, it gives a new character at once to the school and the school-room, and they contemplate it with pleasure instead of dread.

It will also tend to accustom the pupils to recite before strangers, and help them to get rid of that timidity and reserve which, if not early removed, may prove a serious hindrance to their success in many pursuits in after life.

While it will be advisable to assign one or more schools to each member of the committee for the purpose of visiting and general supervision, it is very desirable that all the schools should be visited at least once a term by the *same* person or persons, so that a comparison can be instituted between the different teachers and schools, and the official reports and returns be made out more understandingly. The trustees and parents of each district should be invited to accompany the committee on their visits; and it will be well to encourage the teachers to visit each other's schools with a few of their most advanced scholars.

In visiting schools, whether by the whole board, sub-committee, or individually, the following are among the objects which deserve attention:

The condition of the school-house and appurtenances; its location; size and condition of yard and out-buildings; construction, size, outward appearance, and state of repair of building; condition and size of entries, and whether furnished with scraper, mat, hooks and shelves for hats and outer garments, water-pail, cup, broom, duster, etc.; dimensions of school-room and its condition as to light, whether too much or too little; as to the air, pure or impure; as to temperature, whether too high or too low; modes of ventilation, whether by lowering or raising upper or lower sash, by opening into attic, by flue or otherwise; whether heated by close or open stove, fireplace, furnace or steam; construction and arrangement of seats and desks; whether all the scholars, and especially the younger ones, are comfortably seated, with backs to lean against, and with their feet resting on the floor, and all facing the teacher; whether there is a platform where the teacher can overlook the whole school, and aisles to allow of his passing to every scholar, to give such instruction in his seat, as may be necessary, whether there is a place to arrange the classes for recitation, and accommodations for visitors, etc.

The school register should be called for to see if it is properly kept; and such particulars, as the number and names of the scholars, their age, parents, attendance and studies, should be gleaned as will enable them to speak on the importance of regular and punctual attendance, to expose the evils of the contrary practice, and to commend before the whole school those who are among the most regular. An inspection of the register will oftentimes inform the committee what children are not connected with the school, and a kind and timely call, a word with the parents or guardian, may save such children from ignorance, and the community from its consequences.

In this connection a word should be said in reference to the school census. As soon as the census returns are delivered to the committee, they should be examined with a view to find out who are the regular absentees from school and where they live. Effort should then be made by the committee to secure their attendance. So far as it is possible a careful comparison should be made of the school register and these census returns, so that each may correct the other and thus the committee become possessed of reliable information in regard to the matter of attendance.

The committee should inquire into the number of classes, and the studies they pursue. Such exercises should be called for as will exhibit the proficiency of the pupils, and the methods of instruction adopted by the teacher, and will also enable the committee to judge of the tact of the teacher in imparting information. The teacher, in justice to himself and his pupils, should be allowed to conduct some of the exercises himself, and in his usual manner, as the scholars (if not used to being visited by strangers) will be less timid when examined by him, and the committee will have a better opportunity to see his mode of instruction. But the committee should also ask questions, and, in some cases, take the conduct of the class into their own hands.

When a regular examination is to be had in order to determine the proficiency of the pupils, or the extent of their progress, it will be well to place in the hands of the more advanced scholars written or printed questions, to be answered in writing, while the examination of other classes is going forward. And the same or similar questions should be asked in every school visited, and the answers will be, to some extent, an unexceptionable standard of comparison for both the teachers and the schools.

The committee should be careful to notice the manner in which the pupils spell and read. In reading, especially, there is great carelessness in many of our schools. They should also observe the teacher's manners and mode of governing. If the school is not provided with the proper blackboards, maps, and other necessary apparatus, by proper remarks on their uses and importance, they may be the means of inducing the district to procure them.

Such inquiries should be made as will show how far the rules and regulations of the school committee as to teachers, books, the cleanliness and preservation of the school-house, the manners of the pupils, etc., are observed.

The two distinct purposes of visiting,—inspection and examination,– should be kept constantly in mind, and as far as possible the two should not be allowed to be mingled. The best results will be secured by keeping them well separated, since the methods and means adapted to the one are seldom fitted for the other.

Great care should be taken in all cases not to wound unnecessarily the feelings of teacher or pupils, and commendation should be bestowed wherever it is deserved. It is better to err on the side of praise rather than on that of censure.

Selecting text-books. The schools have heretofore suffered much from the great variety of text-books used, even in the same schools. It has rendered classification impossible, and whenever a scholar changed his district or his school, a new set of books was to be purchased, or a new element of confusion was introduced. Uniformity should be established in the schools of a town at least. In regard to the selection, the committee are entitled to the advice of the commissioner, and the benefit of his experience; and it is expected that they in turn will co-operate with him in such measures as he may recommend, or adopt, to secure a uniformity of books in the State.

But no rule which a committee may adopt as to the books to be used should be so framed or construed as to prevent a teacher from using explanations or illustrations to be found in other books upon any particular subject, or to interfere with the use of all proper reference books by both teacher and pupils. In arithmetic and algebra it will be a profitable exercise for the teacher to give the pupils for solution questions and problems from other books besides the prescribed ones.

No book should be introduced into any public school by the committee, containing any passage or matter reflecting in the least degree upon any religious sect, or which any religious sect would be likely to consider offensive.

In all cases where a change in text-books is contemplated, a written notice to that effect must be given at a regular meeting of the committee, before the action is taken. The vote may be taken at any meeting thereafter, provided suitable time has intervened. Where a book has been adopted for introduction on or after a certain date, the vote can be rescinded any time before that date, but not otherwise.

As to the mode of supplying text-books, it is suggested that where it is possible, some person be procured to act as agent for the sale of text-books, as in that way a great saving in the cost can be effected. It is also recommended that the question of "free text-books," or their supply at the expense of the town, be considered and discussed, as it is believed that this is a full solution of this much vexed problem in school affairs. It has had a favorable trial already in two towns of this State, besides in many other places.

Rules and Regulations. The school committee should prescribe a system of rules and regulations respecting the age, admission, attendance, classification, studies, discipline and instruction of pupils, in all the schools; the examination and duties of teachers; the kind of books to be used, etc. No town should be without such rules.

The age for admission should be uniform in all the districts of a town, as otherwise some districts may have the advantage over others in the apportionment of the public money; but there is no law to prevent the admission of children under five, nor to compel a committee to allow them to enter at that age. The whole matter is left to the discretion of the committee.

In the matter of classification, number and kind of studies and gradation, the schools need and, to accomplish anything, must have the guidance and care of the committee. The law no longer establishes the minimum range of studies, hence, unless the committee acts, there is no authority to decide what shall be, or what shall not be, taught. It is therefore a very important duty for each committee to decide what studies shall be introduced and to what extent they shall be taught. Only as this duty is thoroughly performed will our schools be capable of making any permanent progress. Even the ungraded schools are capable of great improvement in this direction, and a course of study will be found appended to these remarks, which may at least serve as a basis for such a course as it may be deemed best to adopt. While the law plainly gives to the committee absolute power to determine the studies to be pursued, still the committee should be ever ready to heed all reasonable requests of parents and guardians for such deviations therefrom, as the best interests of their children seem to require. What shall be adopted? how far the schools shall go? is wholly within the province of the committee, who will doubtless seek to be governed in that matter by the dominant sentiment of their constituents. Practically the law allows each community to provide just such facilities for the education of its children as it desires.

In the matter of discipline it is suggested that the regulations of the committee should provide clearly for the exercise by the teacher of all proper authority over the pupil, not only during school hours, but whenever he is on school premises, and while on his way to and from school.

The attention of the teachers and pupils should be regularly called to the rules and regulations, and violations thereof should not only not be winked at, but made a matter of serious treatment.

The question of what holidays shall be observed by the schools, and of closing the schools for the purpose of allowing teachers to attend institutes and visit other schools, is one that belongs to the committee under this general provision of the law; and the committee should attend to it. Of course on all holidays established by State law the schools should not be kept. For all other cases the rule must be the voice of the committee.

Apportioning Money. The committee, having ascertained what they can depend upon from the State treasury, the town, registry and other taxes, and having reserved an amount sufficient to defray the expense of printing their report and other necessary contingent expenses, must apportion it on or before the first Monday in July in each year, according to law, and give immediate notice of the amounts of said apportionment to the several trustees. But they are not authorized to pay out or give an order to any district which has not maintained a school for at least six months during the year preceding, except in cases where the school was suspended by the committee for want of pupils. The law makes a district's complying with this provision for one year, a prerequisite to its receiving any money the next year.

Where a school is suspended for lack of the requisite number of pupils, it will usually be found best the first year to set apart for such district a portion of the amount usually allotted, out of which can be paid the expenses incurred in providing school privileges for the children of that district. After the first year the matter will be determined by the facts as they shall appear. In cases of these districts the committee have full power to either send the children to other districts, which they can do without any payment of tuition, or to send to another town and pay tuition. They are also authorized to pay for their transportation to and from school, if their judgment so dictates.

Attention is specially called to the absolute requirement of the law that the committee shall not allow districts to carry forward unexpended balances from one year to another.

The committee are not to give orders on the school fund any faster than they are satisfied that it is actually expended. The times and manner of payment, with the above restrictions, are at the discretion of the committee.

Where the town system prevails there will be no necessity for any such apportionment as above, but such allotment to the several schools, or division of the funds, as shall provide for all of the schools equal advantages and facilities, especially in regard to length of term. A committee, however, has no right to expend more than the amount appropriated by the town.

The committee will find it greatly to their convenience to keep a regular set of accounts. A separate account should be opened with each school or school district, in which the district or school should be from time to time credited with the money apportioned to it, and then charged with the orders which have been given to it.

Another account should be kept by entering all the sums of money appropriated to schools on one side, and all orders given, on the other, which will show at any time the balance under the committee's control.

Returns. By the Public Statutes, chapter 55, section 5, trustees are to make returns to the school committee, at such time and in such form as the committee or commissioner may prescribe. These returns must be made in season to enable the committee to digest them, and prepare their return to the commissioner by July 1st, for which returns the commissioner will furnish forms. The attention of committees is particularly directed to this part of the law, for experience has shown that the incompleteness and inaccuracy of our statistics is due primarily to the failure of the committees to secure proper returns from the trustees and teachers. There is no excuse for such neglect, and every trustee and teacher should be firmly held to a strict compliance with this requirement. The committee are also, at the annual town meeting, to make a written or printed report to the town, of all their doings, the condition of the schools, plans for their improvement, etc. Until the above return and one or more copies of the above report are sent to the commissioner, the town's share of the State appropriation is withheld in accordance with the provisions of the law.

The committee are authorized to reserve enough (not exceeding $40.) out of the school money to print their reports, and no action or vote of the town can take away this authority from the committee. It is believed that no part of the school expenditure will do more good and tend more to keep up an interest in the schools than this, and it is hoped that every committee will always make their report in print.

The committee must aid in organizing districts, by giving the notice for the first meeting. And when there are no trustees, or when the trustees neglect to call meetings, the committee must call them, in the same manner and for the same purposes as the trustee would have called them. The notice may be signed by either the chairman or clerk of the committee, the same as in the case of other official documents issued by the committee.

Any district may vote to devolve upon the committee, with their consent, the whole management of their schools; and in that case, the committee will exercise in that district all the powers which the district itself might exercise; keep the school, have the custody of the school-house, etc.

Gradation of schools. The school committee cannot compel a district to establish graded schools, but they can promote a gradation of schools, or a separation of the younger and the older scholars, or the primary and advanced studies into distinct schools or departments. By such a separation of pupils and instruction a great saving of time and expense is secured, while great benefits are derived by the children. Such a policy should be adopted, as a rule, in preference to the division of a district, where the children have become too numerous for one school.

Where the schools are so divided or graded, the determination of the grades and the promotion from one grade to another are in the hands of the committee.

Whenever the schools of a town are managed independent of districts, a sufficient number of schools of different grades should be established by the committee, at convenient locations, varying the studies pursued according to the circumstances of the population.

The union of two or more adjacent districts, where there are sufficient pupils for the purpose of establishing a secondary or grammar school for the older and more advanced pupils of each district, can be secured to advantage in almost every town, and this phase of the subject should receive the attention of the committees, as it is to them that the people naturally look for suggestions in these matters.

In towns where there are compact villages or communities evening schools should receive the attention of the committee, and efforts should be made to secure from the town specific appropriations for their support. In a manufacturing centre they are a necessary factor in any system of public instruction, and the State now makes an annual appropriation for their support. In all evening schools supported in part by the public money, the question of the qualification of the teachers is in the hands of the committee.

Records. At the first meeting of the year the new members of the committee should have a warrant or certificate of their election from the town clerk, which it would be well to have entered upon the record book, followed by the record of the engagement. The first business should be to organize for the year by the election of chairman and clerk and if the town has not elected a superintendent, to appoint one.

The clerk should *make a full* record of all transactions of the committee, including the motions negatived, as well as those adopted, as parties may be interested, and have a right to appeal in many cases, from a negative vote as well as from an affirmative one. In cases of notices of proposed changes in text-books it would be well in all cases to copy them upon the records.

All changes in the boundaries of the districts must be immediately reported to the town clerk by the clerk of the committee.

When it can be conveniently done, the minutes of the proceedings, as drawn out by the clerk, should be read in open meeting, or at the next meeting, for correction if necessary. Misunderstandings may thus be prevented.

The clerk should always record the names of the members of the committee present at each meeting. He should also keep copies of all abstracts, and all reports made to the commissioner, so that the committee may have them for future reference and comparison.

SCHOOL SUPERINTENDENTS.

By the new act a town may elect at its annual town meeting, or failing to do so, its school committee must appoint, a superintendent of schools. The town council has no voice in the election of superintendent, except in those cases where it has been so provided by special act. Vacancies in this office are to be filled by the committee until the next town meeting. The superintendent will perform such duties and exercise such powers as the committee may assign him.

While great good may be accomplished by the appointment of some qualified person especially to supervise the schools, it was not intended that the creation of the office of town superintendent should relieve the members of the school board from an active participation in this work. The school law renders this duty obligatory upon all the members of the school committee, and for their services they should receive a proper compensation. A town officer should be personally familiar with all the schools of the town ; but this he cannot be, if he delegates the whole duty of visiting and supervision to some other person. In those towns where the school committee and superintendent exercise this mutual oversight, there is a natural and necessary concurrence of opinion as to the merits or demerits of school operations, and the most thorough harmony of sentiment with respect to methods of improvement. Hence, school committees are urged to an increase rather than a diminution, of personal attention to each school, even where the town enjoys the full labors of an efficient town superintendent.

The law provides that the town shall fix the salary of the superintendent, but justice and propriety both seem to demand that the body which determines the amount and character of the labor should also determine the salary; and if the towns would refer this matter to their committees, it is believed an increased efficiency in the service would be the result.

As the present law provides for the election of superintendent by the people, or his appointment by the committee, it should be said that the legal status of the superintendent depends somewhat on the nature of his appointment. If he is elected by the people he is classed as a civil officer and must himself be a qualified elector, and he derives his general power from the people, and may, in cases where specific duties are assigned him by the committee, act independently of them until such assignment is withdrawn. But if he is appointed by the committee he is not a civil officer as before, but simply an agent of the committee and wholly subject to their direction and control. He need not be a voter or even a resident, and a woman would be as eligible as a man. In this case all of his acts would be subject to revision by the committee. The latter plan is recommended as productive of the most harmony of administration, and the most beneficial results.

The following suggestions are submitted concerning town superintendents:

1. Each town should have a good superintendent of schools, elected by the school committee.

2. Where one town is not able to secure such an officer, two contiguous towns should unite in electing

the same officer for both towns, his salary to be fixed by the school committees of the towns, and paid by both towns, jointly.

3. This officer should be paid such a salary as will enable him to devote the whole, or a large portion, of his time to the work.

4. He should visit and inspect the schools, examine the pupils, make promotions, suggest improvements in instruction and government, hold teachers' meetings and public meetings in the different sections of the town, and in every way foster and encourage the work of public education.

5. He should examine the teachers, in connection with the school committee if possible, and should sign and annul certificates only by the approval of the majority of the school board.

6. He should allow no text-books to be used in the schools, except such as are approved by the school board of the town.

7. He should see that the rules and regulations of the school committee are honored and enforced, and should make a written report on the condition of the schools and school property to the school committee at each quarterly meeting or oftener,—such report to be embodied in the report of the school committee, to be printed and distributed annually, among the citizens and families of the town.

BRIEF SYNOPSIS OF DUTIES OF SCHOOL COMMITTEES.

1. The examination of teachers.

2. The granting of certificates to teachers and the power to annul the same.

3. The location of all school-houses.

4. The visiting of the schools.

5. The adoption of all rules and regulations relating to the management of schools.

6. The suspension of pupils from schools.

7. The adoption of new text-books by a vote of two-thirds of the whole school board.

8. The apportionment of the public money to the several school districts.

9. The contracting with teachers and the management of all school affairs, when so authorized by the town.

10. The written approval of all district taxes, and of all plans for building and repairing school-houses.

11. The drawing of all orders on the town treasurer for school money.

12. The annual division of unexpended school money among the districts.

13. An annual report to the town, to be read in open town meeting, or printed for distribution.

14. A statistical return to the commissioner of public schools, on or before the first day of July in each year, including a copy of the above report.

15. The formation of all new school districts, the alteration or discontinuing of school districts, and the approval of the formation of associate, joint and consolidated districts.

16. The holding of at least four meetings in each year.

17. The appointment of a town superintendent of schools, when that officer is not elected at the annual town meeting.

18. The calling of district meetings in certain cases.

DISTRICTS.

There are three provisions made in the law for uniting districts. Any two or more districts may form a partial union for the purpose of supporting a higher, secondary or grammar school.

Any contiguous districts in adjoining towns may be united by the school committees, and adjoining districts in the same town may consolidate themselves subject to the approval of the committee. When united they constitute a single district, and their affairs must be managed in the same way as if originally one district; but they will be entitled to the same proportion of public money they would receive if not united.

A district cannot vote to dissolve itself. Such a vote will be wholly null and void. It can be dissolved by the school committee alone, who also have the sole power to create new districts and change the boundaries of those already existing.

Moderator. The moderator of a district meeting is now an annual officer and is to be elected with the other officers at the annual meeting. He need not be engaged. He will preside at all district meetings, both annual and special. If he is absent, a moderator *pro tem* should be chosen. It is the business of the moderator to preside over the meeting, guide its business, and preserve order. While he will usually be justified in obeying common parliamentary rules in the exercise of his duties, still the meeting is superior to any rules, and if an appeal from any of his rulings is taken, it must be allowed, and, if sustained, the will of the meeting obeyed. The moderator is entitled to vote only as any other voter may vote. He has no casting vote. In receiving votes for any officer or on any question, the moderator has no right to reject any man's vote. He is in no sense the judge; but he can insist upon knowing how he votes, and have his name and vote recorded by the clerk, so that, if a question arises, it can be settled by the proper authorities. In any case of doubtful legality, or of contested elections, a moderator would do well to have such a record of the voters and their votes made as the law provides for. The moderator has power to administer the oath of office to all the other officers, either at the meeting, or afterwards.

It is the moderator's duty to maintain order in a meeting and in case persons present refuse to conduct themselves properly, he should order them to leave the meeting. Provision is made in the law whereby town constables, upon the tender of the required fee, are obliged to be present at any school or other lawfully assembled meeting, and they are authorized to arrest without a warrant, and detain for six hours, any person found unlawfully disturbing such meeting.

Clerk. The district clerk should be engaged by the moderator and make a record of it. If not present at the time of his election so as to be engaged in open meeting, he should be engaged before entering upon the duties of his office. A clerk *pro tem.* must be engaged before he enters upon the duties the same as the regular clerk. When engaged, the clerk may engage all other district officers, and should enter all such cases in his record book.

When a trustee, treasurer, etc., is elected, the clerk should make out and sign and seal a warrant or certificate of his election, upon which he may be engaged. [See forms.]

The clerk should, at the request of any person interested, record a motion which is negatived, as well as a motion passed, as in many cases a person may be entitled to an appeal. And he should record the number and names of the voters on request, and in general he should endeavor to make his minutes as full as possible, so that they may give the whole history of the meeting.

In the record of every meeting, it would be well for the clerk to state how the meeting was notified, and when and by whom the notices were posted up. In many cases, at some distance of time, it might be important to know how the meeting was notified, and the evidence of it should not be left to depend upon mere recollection. The record of the clerk is made *prima facie* evidence that the meeting was legally notified, and inhabitants of the district can be admitted to prove the notice. But it would be easy and best to preserve one of the original notices themselves, especially when a tax is to be voted.

It would be well also for the clerk, at the close of every meeting, to read aloud the minutes he has made of the proceedings, so that any mistake may be corrected at the time. Errors in the record may be subsequently corrected and the true record established by proper evidence.

The clerk is to procure a bound record book at the expense of the district. For any wilful neglect or refusal to perform any duty, he is liable to indictment, and the supreme court would, probably, upon application, compel him by writ of mandamus to perform such duty.

District Treasurer. The treasurer should have a certificate of his election [see form] and be engaged. He need not give bond unless required. But if the district requires him to give bond it should run to the district, and the district should fix the sum and approve of the surety or sureties. [See form.]

His duties are very simple: to keep the district's money if they have any, pay it out to order, and keep proper accounts of it, and exhibit them to the trustees or district when required. He should always make a report at the annual meeting, and a copy of it should be given to the trustees, in order that he may make up his return to the school committee. In case the district hires money the treasurer is the one to sign the note. [See form.]

District Collector. The collector should always be engaged before beginning his duties. If the district requires the collector to give bond, the district should fix the sum, and, as in case of treasurer's bond, it should run to the district; and the district should approve of the surety or sureties. If, however, the district votes to have the town collector act, he is to give bond to the district, satisfactory to the school committee.

If no compensation is agreed upon before the collector is elected, he is entitled by law to five per cent. upon the amount collected. On the other hand a district cannot vote to pay more than five per cent. [See the forms for warrants and tax lists.]

Trustees. One or three trustees are to be appointed by a district at its annual meeting, but the decision, as to one or three, must be made before the election of any. If by any accident an election is not made then, or if a vacancy occurs, the district may elect afterwards. Trustees hold their offices until their successors are qualified, and can only be removed from their office, before the expiration of the term for which they were elected, for cause, and after notice and trial.

If there are three trustees, a majority can act, but the action of only one would be void. "Where a body or board of officers is constituted by law to perform a trust for the public, or to execute a power or perform a duty prescribed by law, it is not necessary that all should concur in the act done. The act of the majority is the act of the body. And where all have due notice of the time and place of meeting in the manner prescribed by law, if so prescribed—or by the rules and regulations of the body itself, if there be any,—otherwise if reasonable notice is given, and no practice or unfair means are used to prevent all from attending and participating in the proceeding, it is no objection that all the members do not attend, if there be a quorum." [21 Pick. 28.] All business must be done at a meeting of the board, of which due notice was given to all the members.

The trustees must employ the teacher. In employing a teacher or assistant teacher, trustees should be cautious to employ no one who has not a legal certificate, and not to employ one after notice that his certificate is annulled, as in such a case the trustees would be held personally liable for the teacher's wages. The trustee has no power either to annul a certificate, or dismiss a teacher before the expiration of the time for which he was hired. The trustees should see that the teacher keeps a proper record of attendance, as is required by the authorities, in order that the district may receive its due portion of school money next year; and when the school is over, the register should be deposited with the committee. They should require the teacher to furnish them with such items of information as are necessary to make out their annual report to the town committee, which report should be made on the first of May, or sooner if the school is out, or at such time as the committee shall fix. Forms for these reports will be furnished to the districts, and can be obtained from the committee or from the superintendent.

If trustees appropriate any of the public money to pay a teacher not legally examined, they are liable to a penalty. The uses for which the public money may be employed are teachers' wages, fuel, janitor's service and necessary books for indigent pupils, with some other current expenses.

If any scholars from without the town or State, can more conveniently attend school in any other district and desire to do so, the trustee of the district is authorized to make the necessary arrangements, subject to the approval of the school committee. They should also take care that the school is kept in a house which will not be disapproved of by the committee of the town. To that end the trustees are authorized to make repairs that are immediately necessary for the preservation of the property and the maintenance of the school, without a vote of the district, and the district would be obliged to pay for such repairs. While the control and care of the school property is in the hands of the trustee he has no right to remove or dispose of any of it, except by vote of the district. As the custodian of the school-house he may allow its use for purposes connected with education, even against the wish of the district, but he cannot be compelled to allow its use for such a purpose, provided he does not think it best. Nor *can* he allow its use for religious meetings, if a single tax-payer objects. If, however, the school-house has been *given* to the district under certain conditions, the trustee will be bound thereby.

Trustees should regard the visiting of the schools as one of the most important of their duties, which should by no means be neglected.

When a district is organized and has trustees, they are the only district officers authorized to notify the annual and special district meetings, and they cannot delegate this power, and if there is no district school-house, or place appointed by the district, they are to fix the place of meeting. A special meeting may be called within the time fixed for another meeting, if the length of time will permit, provided the object thereof is different. If the trustees on application neglect to call a meeting, the school committee may call it.

Trustees, for refusal to discharge any duty, call a meeting, assess a tax, etc., etc., are liable to a penalty. And the supreme court would probably, upon application, compel any school officer, by writ of mandamus, to discharge any duty plainly imposed on him by the law.

Trustees should encourage meetings of teachers in their neighborhoods for mutual improvement, and also insist upon their attendance upon all institutes and other similar gatherings, and as far as possible aid them in going to and from such meetings. If any teacher neglects or refuses to attend a teachers' institute, when organized under proper auspices, and when he can conveniently, it should be regarded as a sign of unfitness for the place. No one is so well qualified, as not to be able to learn from his fellows many useful hints as to methods of teaching, books, etc., and no one should be unwilling or too proud to learn.

If the committee authorize schools to be closed, the trustee has no power to prevent it and cannot compel a teacher to make up such days or legal holidays, except by special agreement.

Trustees have no authority to make any rules and regulations in regard to the school, such as, times of sessions, recesses, studies, etc. They can however fix the limits of the school terms, subject to some general rules of the committee. And in this connection they should be very particular to notify the committee or superintendent of the beginning and ending of *every* term, in order that the schools may be properly visited.

Trustees should see that an inventory of all the maps, books and other property belonging to the district, is made from time to time, and preserved among the papers of the district.

Every district should possess a dictionary, maps of

the State, the United States, and of the town (if there is one), a globe, and such other apparatus and works of reference as the means of the district, or the public spirit thereof, will allow. With the aid now given by the State, no district need be without these essentials to a good school.

Trustees should recollect that in order to obtain from the school committee any order for money, they must have made a proper return from their district, for the year ending on the first of May previous, and must also furnish to the committee a certificate that the "teachers' money," (that is, the money which the district received from the town treasurer as their part of the State appropriation,) for the year ending the first of May previous, has been applied to the wages of teachers, and to no other purpose whatever.

The return of the district should include the whole time during which any portion of the public money has been used to support the school, and should include *all* expenditures for the benefit of the school, whether from district funds or any other source, and should state *all* the sources whence the moneys were obtained.

Trustees are cautioned in reference to these returns, that the committees have been instructed to refuse to draw their orders except upon the receipt of the proper return fully and accurately made out.

If a trustee removes from the district he ceases to be trustee from the date of his actual removal, and therefore cannot act at all as trustee after that date.

In assessment of taxes, which *must* be done by the trustees, and not by assessors, the trustee has no power to remit, or alter valuation. He has no discretionary power in the matter.

Where the district maintains an evening school, the trustee would sustain exactly the same relation to it, as to the day schools.

Qualifications for office. In order to be eligible to any district office, a person must possess the qualifications of a voter; and any voter may be elected to any district office.

It is sufficient if the person elected have the qualifications of a voter at the time of his election. He will not afterwards lose the office by simply losing his qualification to vote.

Engagement. Every officer must be engaged by some one duly authorized to administer oaths before he enters upon the discharge of his duties. The following officers may administer the oath to school district officers: the moderator of the district, district clerk, town clerk, president of town council, trial justice, justices of the peace, and public notaries. When an officer is engaged at any other time than in the district meeting, he should always receive a written certificate of his engagement. [See form.]

The same person may hold more than one office at the same time, where the duties of the two do not conflict, or where the law does not make one officer responsible to the other: that is, one person may be both moderator and trustee or collector; but the two offices of moderator and clerk cannot be filled by the same person at the same time, neither the offices of trustee and collector, nor those of collector and treasurer.

Vacancies in office are always created by absolute removal from the district, and an officer has no authority to act after such removal. But great care should be taken before proceeding to fill any such vacancies, to see that the evidence of the removal and consequent vacancy is incontestible; for there is often a temporary removal or absence which could not be regarded as a legal removal, and any attempt to fill the so-called vacancy would lead to difficulty.

Resignations should always be given in writing, addressed either to the clerk of the district, or the trustee. Oral resignations are so liable to be the source of misunderstanding that they should never be used. A resignation can be withdrawn any time before it has been accepted, either formally, or by filling the vacancy.

All district officers are to be elected annually, but *all* school officers, whether town or district, will hold over till their successors are not only elected, but qualified. A pecuniary interest in the introduction of any school text-book disqualifies any school officer whatever from continuing in his office.

Voting. To enable a person to vote in a district meeting, he must reside in the district and possess the qualifications requisite to entitle him to have his name put upon the voting list of the town at that time; but his name need not actually be upon the list. To vote as a tax-payer, a man must pay, or be able to pay, a town and State tax of at least one dollar.

Tax paying residents alone have the right to vote on questions involving the expenditure of money, but a non-resident, though a tax-payer, has no vote at all. Registry voters are qualified to vote for one year from the time of the payment of their registry tax.

If a person residing in a joint district moves from one *town* to the other, he loses his vote in that district, till he has gained it in the other town.

Certificate voters, so-called, cannot vote for school district officers.

Meetings. As to notifying meetings, see chapter 52, section 5. A meeting called by only one notice is never legal, nor where the notice is signed by any other persons than the trustees or school committee; all business transacted at an illegal meeting is void.

The notice for an *annual* meeting need not specify any of the items of business. But every notice of a *special* meeting *must* state specifically what business is to be done, or it will be illegal. All notices must be posted at least five days before the meeting. [See form.] When met, the meeting must organize by choosing a moderator and clerk. The moderator need not be engaged. The clerk, whether regular or pro tem, must be engaged before he enters upon the discharge of his duties. He may then engage all other district officers, and his record will be evidence of his own and their engagements. If there is a failure to appoint officers at the annual meeting they may be appointed afterwards, and vacancies may be filled at any time.

If the moderator refuses to put questions to vote, or if he or any other district officer violates the law, he is liable to pay a fine, or to be brought before the Supreme Court and compelled to act.

The annual district meeting is to be in April, but special meetings may be called by the trustees at any time as their judgment may decide. Any legal meeting may adjourn to a specified time, and continue at that adjournment the business which was specified in the call, or which it was proper to consider at the first meeting.

Inhabitants of districts may be witnesses in all cases, and so may prove (if disputed) the legality of the notice and meeting, but the clerk's record that the meeting has been duly notified will be *prima facie* evidence of the fact.

Quorum. It has been repeatedly decided in the courts of England and this country, that at common law, where there is no statute provision, when a meeting of a corporation, consisting of an indefinite number of persons, (as towns, districts, etc.,) is properly notified, no particular number is necessary to form a quorum, but a majority of those present may act.

To require a majority of the voters of the district, would in many cases prevent the doing of any business at all. And to fix any particular number would be difficult, because there are some districts where this number would be more than the whole number of voters. The law has therefore required the notice of the meeting to be given with great particularity, and then presumes that every voter, who does not attend, assents to what is done by those present.

At the same time it will not be advisable to proceed in any matter of importance, such as laying a tax, etc., unless a respectable number of voters attend.

Order of business. A district has full power to make its own rules of order, and any district meeting is competent to overrule any decision or ruling of the moderator, and he is bound to conform to their votes in such matters.

In the election of officers where only one person is nominated, it is generally enough to call for all in favor of his election to say, "aye," and all opposed to say, "no." If there is the least doubt in the moderator's mind as to the vote, he should take it again, by show of hands. Where two or more persons are nominated for the same office, a ballot should *always* be taken by the moderator. If a ballot is called for on any question and the call is seconded, the moderator should put the question to the meeting, whether they will have a ballot. If the call is not seconded he can act his own pleasure. If a request is made for a record of the voters and how they voted, it must be taken, but the request must be made before the voting begins. A district may therefore reconsider a vote at any time as well upon the motion of one who did not vote for it, as upon that of one who did; and the district may also rescind any vote at any time, before any contract has been made under it. But after a contract has been made, or an individual has incurred any expense or liabilities in consequence of a vote of the district, they cannot with justice rescind it. And if it is rescinded, they will be held liable to make good all damages and losses incurred.

A subsequent meeting cannot by vote legalize the illegal action of a preceding meeting.

TAXATION.

General provisions. The districts have power to build, purchase, hire and repair school-houses, provide blackboards, maps, furniture, and all necessary and useful appendages. The law gives them a general power to tax for school purposes. They may tax to pay rent of a hired house. They may also tax to repair a hired house, provided they have a valid lease of it for a definite period. They may also tax to maintain a day or evening school, but they cannot impose any tuition tax or rate bill on the resident pupils. And to guard against any abuse of this power, the tax must be approved by the school committee, and the plans for building and repairs must also be approved by the committee, or, on appeal, by the commissioner; but this approval is simply an approval of the *amount* of tax, and not an endorsement of the accuracy or validity of the tax bill. And in all cases of levying taxes, it is necessary to vote either a sum certain, or a sum not less than a certain sum, and not more than a certain sum, or a certain percentage on the valuation of the ratable property of the district. The amount levied may be greater than the indebtedness of the district. Indeed it is desirable that there should be some funds in the treasury all of the time. Every vote to levy a tax must specify a time when it shall be due, or it will not be collectible.

All taxes must be voted and collected according to the present school act, all the former town and local acts being repealed.

On laying a tax, or on any question relating to the expenditure of money, those only are entitled to vote who shall have paid, or are liable to pay, taxes; and no tax can be assessed or money hired on the credit of the district without the direct vote of the district to that effect.

Assessment of taxes. Unless the district vote to have their tax assessed according to the *next* town valuation, the trustee or trustees must proceed to make out the tax bill according to the *last* town valuation. If there are any complaints of wrong valuation, it would be well for the district to postpone the tax until the *next* town assessment is completed, to give the parties an opportunity to be heard before the town assessors.

There are no such officers recognized by the law as district assessors, and if a district should elect such, and they should assess a tax it could not be collected; nor would a tax be collectible if assessed by trustees, one or all of whom were subsequently found to be disqualified, or illegally elected.

A vote to assess by the next town valuation is the only way for a district to avail itself of any increase in the taxable property of the district. The trustee, either by himself or by assessors, has no right to make a new valuation for individuals, or for the whole district indeed, apart from the rest of the town.

If any property within the district is assessed to any person, together with property out of the district, so that there is no separate valuation of that portion which may lie within the district lines, and in the other cases referred to in chap. 54, sec. 2, the trustees must first endeavor to agree with the parties interested as to the valuation of the property, and in case they cannot agree they must then apply in writing to one or more of the town assessors, living out of the district, stating the names of the parties so situated; and the assessor will immediately issue a notice, and at the expiration of the ten days, proceed to decide and apportion the valuation, and in his return to the trustee he should certify over his official signature to all of the material facts. As the assessor is called upon to act in these cases solely upon business of the district, his fees should be paid by the district.

The following is an abstract of the general tax laws of the State; but a trustee or assessor, before proceeding to act, should always inquire if they have been altered or amended.

In assessing a tax, real and personal estate must be valued separately, and put in separate columns, and the assessors must distinguish those who give in a list. Taxes on real estate must be assessed to the owner or tenant for life, and separate tracts or parcels should be separately described and valued, as far as practicable. They should not be assessed against a person deceased, but may be assessed to the estate or heirs of the deceased until the assessors have notice of a division, and each heir is liable for the whole tax. If a tax be assessed on real estate by mistake to a person not the owner thereof, the tax may be collected from such real estate, provided it can be identified, and that the real owner has notice of the assessment.

If any real estate has changed owners since the last town valuation, it, of course, must be assessed to the actual owners at the time the school-tax bill is made out. This is the reasonable construction of the law. If the new owner resides out of the district, the purchase does not carry the property out of the district too. It is still taxable where it is situated.

Persons must be taxed for personal property according to their residence for the greater portion of the twelve months next preceding the first day of April in each year, unless otherwise provided. But a person moving into the State will be taxable in the town and district where he resides when the tax is assessed. If a person moves out of the State before the assessment, he is not liable. The general rule as to taxation is, that personal property shall be taxed to the owner where he resides, and real estate where it lies. A few exceptions from this rule, made by statute, are hereafter referred to.

Buildings on leased land, where the lease is recorded, are to be deemed real estate, but in other cases they would be regarded as personal property. Standing wood to be cut and removed, if there is no deed of the land, is to be regarded as personal property. It has been decided in Massachusetts, that a person residing on land ceded to the United States, and where the State has only reserved a right of serving process, is not taxable. (8 Mass. 72; 1 Metcalf, 680.) Machinery in cotton and woolen factories, merchandise, stock in trade, lumber and coal, stock in livery stables, being permanently located in any town, are to be taxed in the towns where located, in the same manner as if the owner resided there.

Personal property in trust, the income of which is to be paid to some other person, must be assessed to the trustee in the town where such other person resides, if in the State, but if such person lives out of the State, then it is to be taxed where the trustee, executor, etc., resides.

Personal property in the hands of the executors; guardians, etc., is to be taxed to them in the town where the deceased dwelt, or the ward resides, if a resident of this State; but if not, then in the town where the guardian resides.

Collection of taxes. The taxes must be collected by the district collector, or the town collector, if the district so votes. A tax paid to the treasurer or any other person, does not release the party. If the town collector serves, he does not need to be engaged as district collector.

Before the collector proceeds to the collection of the taxes he should see that the provisions of the law regarding the assessment have been complied with.

The mode of distraining and selling personal property is pointed out in the general statutes. The mode of notifying and selling land for taxes is also prescribed by law. In either of the above cases the collector should be very particular to follow the exact letter of the law, keeping *within*, rather than overstepping, its bounds. If a person is taxed for more than one parcel of land, the whole tax may be collected out of any one parcel, and the real estate is liable for the tax on both real and personal property. A tax warrant remains in force until the whole tax is collected, even though a second or third tax may have been levied in the meantime.

If the collector dies, resigns or is removed, the new collector, in order to complete the collection, should receive a new warrant. The oath of the collector is admitted to prove a demand. Any district may offer a deduction to those who pay on or before a certain time, or impose a percentage on those who do not, not to exceed the rate of twelve per cent. per annum.

All property which is exempted from attachment by the laws of this State, or of the United States, such as the uniform, arms, ammunition and equipments of an officer or private in the militia, household furniture, family stores, tools, etc., cannot be distrained for taxes.

Owners of real estate or buildings sold for taxes, may redeem within one year after sale, on paying to the purchaser the amount paid therefor, with twenty per cent. in addition.

Any person neglecting to appear before the assessor, after notice given, has no remedy. Any tax or assessment not appealed from cannot be questioned in court afterwards. Provision is made for correcting errors and re-assessing a tax by application to the commissioner.

All claims for abatement of taxes must be made to the district, who alone have authority to make the same; save in cases where the plea is based upon a change of boundaries, when an appeal is allowed to the committee, or the commissioner.

[See the forms and notes, and especially the notes to the form of a vote for laying a tax.]

TEACHERS.

Every teacher is required to keep a record of all the scholars attending the school, their sex, names, ages, names of parents or guardians, the time when they enter and leave school, their daily attendance, and the dates when the school is visited by the commissioner, committee, or trustees. These registers should be furnished by the committee, to whom they are sent by the commissioner. From the register the teacher must furnish the trustees with such information as may be necessary to make the returns required by the school committee.

It would be well for the teacher to inform the committee of the time of commencing and closing his school, in order that they may know when to visit it, as the trustees sometimes neglect this duty.

It is important that the register be correctly kept, and the average rightly calculated, as upon that depends in part the amount of money the district will receive next year. Moreover accuracy in all of the statistics is of the highest importance, and the teachers are especially directed to follow carefully the directions to be found in the registers.

The teacher should assist the trustees by all the means in his power, in making the proper returns, as upon their accuracy and fullness may depend the success or failure of many provisions of the law, as well as the wisdom of future alterations of it. Full directions for making out these returns are to be found on all the blanks which are furnished, and these directions should be strictly followed.

The teacher should conform to all regulations of the school committee, in regard to hours, studies, discipline, text-books, etc., as for any violation of them, his certificate may be annulled, or he may be dismissed. He may, (if the school committee by regulation authorize it), suspend a scholar temporarily, until a hearing can be had before the committee, in which case he should immediately notify the committee, and the parents or guardian of the child.

The law fixes no minimum standard of qualifications, but it is left for the school committee of each town to determine their own standard. Each teacher should, however, endeavor to add to his acquirements, and should realize that all knowledge is valuable and of use in a school-room.

There is no appeal to the commissioner from a refusal of a committee to grant a certificate.

No member of the committee, or superintendent, or trustee, can teach any school supported wholly or in part by the public moneys, in the town where he resides.

If the teacher has a proper sense of the importance of his position, and conducts himself accordingly, he will secure to himself the affection and respect of the people of his district, by exerting his utmost powers to promote the moral and intellectual advancement, not only of his scholars, but of the community around him. The moral influence he may exert by his example and instructions, can hardly be estimated. And he may, by encouraging lectures and literary meetings, aid in diffusing much useful information.

Moral instruction should by all means be inculcated by the teacher, but yet so as to avoid all sectarian comments or bias.

The rule as laid down in the laws of the State of Massachusetts, while it points out and inculcates the duty of the teacher to give moral instruction, is carefully drawn to avoid giving countenance to any attempt to impart sectarian instruction, and may well be followed in this commonwealth.

"It shall be the duty of the teachers to use their best endeavors to impress upon the minds of the youth committed to their care and instruction, the principles of piety, justice, and a sacred regard to truth, love to their country, humanity and universal benevolence, sobriety, industry, frugality, chastity, moderation, temperance, and those other virtues which are the ornament of human society and the basis upon which a republican constitution is founded; and they shall endeavor to lead their pupils, as their ages and capacities will allow, into a clear understanding of the tendencies of these virtues to preserve and perfect a republican constitution, and secure the blessings of liberty, as well as to promote their own happiness; and also to point out to them the evil tendency of the opposite vices."

Reading the Bible and praying in schools. The constitution and laws of the State give no power to a school committee, nor is there any authority in the State by which the reading of the Bible or praying in school, either at the opening or at the close, can be commanded and enforced. On the other hand, the spirit of the constitution, and the neglect of the law to specify any penalty for so opening or closing a school, or to appoint or allow any officer to take notice of such an act, do as clearly show that there can be no compulsory exclusion of such reading and praying from our public schools. The whole matter must be regulated by the consciences of the teachers and inhabitants of the district, and by the general consent of the community. Statute law and school committees' regulations can enforce neither the use nor disuse of such devotional exercises. School committees may recommend, but they can go no further.

It is believed to be the general sentiment of the people of Rhode Island, that this matter shall be left to the conscience of the teacher; and it is expected that if he read the Bible as an opening exercise, he shall read such parts as are not controverted or disputed, but such as are purely or chiefly devotional; and if he pray at the opening of his school, he shall be very brief, and conform as nearly to the model of the Lord's Prayer as the nature of the case will admit. And in all this he is bound to respect the conscientious scruples of the parents of the children before him, as he would have his own conscientious scruples respected by them in turn; always, of course, taking care that in the means he uses to show his respect for the consciences of others, he does not violate the law of his own conscience.

In regard to the use of the Bible in schools, two observations occur here. If the committee prescribe, or the teacher wishes, to have the Bible read in school, it should not be forced upon any children whose parents have any objections whatever to its use. In most cases the teacher will have no difficulty with the parents on this subject, if he conducts with proper kindness and courtesy. In the next place, no scholars should be required to read the Bible at school, until they have learned to read with tolerable fluency. To use it as a text book for the younger scholars, often has the effect of leading them to look upon it with the same sort of careless disregard, and sometimes dislike, with which they regard their other school-books, instead of that respect and veneration with which this book of books should always be treated and spoken of.

In the last part of this manual will be found certain forms of prayer, which are given, simply as a guide to those who wish to use this service and as an indication of that form which would be generally acceptable to any community. These particular forms are those allowed by law to be used in the public schools of Canada, and are both comprehensive in their scope and appropriate in their diction.

Power to punish. The teacher should maintain a careful supervision over the conduct of his pupils at all times when they are upon the school premises. Recesses and the brief periods at the beginning and close of school, when the children are mingling together in the school yard, are times above all others, when the watchful eye of the teacher should be on the alert. The conduct of pupils on their way to and from school should also not escape the notice of the teacher, though the extent of the teacher's authority to enforce obedience in such circumstances is much more restricted than in cases occurring on the school premises.

This question of the extent of the teacher's authority has been very widely discussed, and has been the subject of many controversies and judicial decisions in various States; and while it is impossible to lay down a rule which shall cover all cases, the general principles have been quite well defined, and were very clearly set forth in a recent case in the Supreme Court of this State where a teacher was sued for damages on account of unlawful and excessive punishment. The court, Mr. Justice Tillinghast presiding, instructed the jury substantially, as follows:

An assault and battery is any unlawful physical force used against the person of another. It matters not how slight or how great the force, so that it be unlawful and wrongful, it is an assault and battery. This defendant is charged with the use of such force against the person of the plaintiff. She admits that she did use physical force against him — that she did punish him with the instrument which she has produced before you, — so that, the force being admitted the first and principal question for you to determine is whether it was unlawful or wrongful. If so, she is guilty as charged. If not, she is not guilty.

The defendant justifies her conduct, or seeks to justify it, on the ground that she was a teacher in a public school; that this plaintiff was a pupil under her charge; and that the only force she used was the infliction of such reasonable and judicious bodily punishment, as she lawfully might inflict for the disobedience and misconduct of the pupil. That a teacher of a public school has the right to inflict corporal punishment upon a pupil, for sufficient cause, is not disputed. He stands, practically, for the time being, in place of the parent, and may lawfully and properly inflict such punishment as may be reasonable and necessary to compel obedience and a due regard for the well-ordering and good government of the school.

Judge Blackstone says, "The master is *in loco parentis*, and has such a *portion* of the powers of the parent committed to his charge as may be necessary to answer the purposes for which he is employed."

Punishment of this sort should, however, be administered with especial care and prudence, and always with temperate zeal and moderation. If in any case the punishment is clearly excessive, it then becomes unjustifiable, and the teacher is liable.

It being admitted then, that the teacher has the right to punish his pupil for acts of misbehavior committed in school, we will enquire as to his right to punish for such acts committed before the school was commenced, or after it was dismissed. Upon this point there is some difference of opinion in the community, but the law seems to be well settled, and is this:—that for such misbehavior out of school as has a direct and immediate tendency to injure the school, to subvert the master's authority, and to beget disorder and insubordination, the teacher may inflict corporal punishment. "It is not misbehavior generally," says ALDIS J., "or towards other persons, or even towards the master in matters in no ways connected with or affecting the school. For as to such matters, committed by the child after his return home from school the parents, and they alone, have the power of punishment." But where the offence has a direct and immediate tendency to injure the school and bring the teacher's authority into contempt, as in this case, when done in the presence of other scholars and of the teacher, and with a design to insult her, she has the right to punish the scholar for such acts, if he comes again to school.

"The misbehavior," says the same Judge, "must not have merely a remote and indirect tendency to injure the school. All improper conduct or language may perhaps have, by influence and example, a remote tendency of that kind. But the tendency of the acts so done out of the teacher's supervision, for which he may punish, must be direct and immediate in their bearing upon the welfare of the school, or the authority of the teacher and the respect due him.

"Cases may readily be supposed which lie very near the line, and it will often be difficult to distinguish between the acts which have such an immediate, and those which have such a remote, tendency. Hence each case must be determined by its peculiar circumstances."

"Acts done to deface or injure the school-room, to destroy the books of scholars, or the books or apparatus for instruction, or the instruments of punishment of the master; language used to other scholars to stir up disorder and insubordination, or to heap odium and disgrace upon the master; writings and pictures placed so as to suggest evil and corrupt language, images and thoughts to the youth who must frequent the school; all such or similar acts tend directly to impair the usefulness of the school, the welfare of the scholars, and the authority of the master. By common consent and by the universal custom in our New England schools, the master has always been deemed to have the right to punish such offences.

"Such power is essential to the preservation of order, decency, decorum and good government in schools."

Of course any direct personal insult or indignity to the teacher, as snow-balling her, stoning her and other like conduct out of school would come within the same rule. The reasonable exercise of the teacher's authority over her pupils both in and out of school, as to those things which pertain directly to the well-being of the school, must be upheld and sustained, or our public school system will prove worse than a failure.

If you find, therefore, that the punishment inflicted by the defendant in this case was either for misconduct committed in school, or out of school, under such circumstances as I have described to you, and that it was not clearly excessive under the circumstances of the case, then the justification set up by defendant is made out, and you will find a verdict of not guilty. If you find that the punishment was wrongfully inflicted, or excessive, then you will find a verdict of guilty and assess such damages in favor of the plaintiff as you think him fairly entitled to.

The jury returned a verdict of NOT GUILTY.

The teacher should remember that while the law holds him responsible for his acts in the school-room, it also protects him while therein employed from all external or unofficial interference. No private person has any right, in any circumstances, to enter a school-room in school hours to make any complaint or to disturb the school in any way. The statute law provides a specific penalty for such an offence.

APPEALS.

The law has wisely provided a cheap and efficient mode of settling all disputes arising under the school-law. It was intended to save the expense of litigation to districts and individuals, and it is believed that it has already had the effect of saving a great expenditure of money in this way, as well as effecting a more speedy settlement of difficulties, which, if continued, would interrupt the harmony of the districts and injure the schools. An appeal may be taken to the commissioner [see the forms], and he will hear the parties without cost, and his decision is to be final as to the facts or merits of the case. When questions of law arise, provision is made for laying them before one of the judges of the Supreme Court, but the judges will not examine or hear the parties upon the facts of the case. When a case is submitted to one of the judges, it has been decided that the commissioner must make a statement of the facts as he finds them to be established by the evidence, and that this statement is to be submitted, and not the evidence itself.

Any party neglecting to appeal from a vote to tax, or an assessment of a tax, cannot question it afterwards, provided the meeting was legally notified, and the tax approved, etc.

It has been settled that an appeal brings the whole question up, and that the commissioner in many cases is not confined to confirming or reversing the proceedings appealed from, but may make a new decision.

All appeals, however, should be taken within a reasonable time, and before any contract is made, or liability incurred, under the vote or act appealed from. If the appeal is not made within such a reasonable time, that circumstance alone will be a sufficient reason for dismissing it. And no appeal will be entertained unless made by the party aggrieved.

Written notice of the appeal should always be sent to the party whose action is appealed from, or to the officer whose title is questioned, and as a rule it is best to send a copy of the appeal itself, as such a course will usually save time.

Deaf, dumb, blind and idiotic. A State school for the deaf has been established in Providence, under the control of the Board of Education. It is a day school, conducted somewhat after the plan of the Horace Mann school in Boston. All residents of the State are entitled to free admission. Provision is also made whereby aid may be given to indigent pupils living out of the city, to enable them to pay their travelling expenses.

In addition to the above an appropriation of six thousand dollars is made annually by the State for the education of the indigent deaf and dumb, blind, and idiotic, at such institutions as the governor may decide upon.

As there are some of these unfortunates in every town in the State, the school committees and friends of education and humanity should look them up and see that they receive the advantages which the State provides so liberally for them.

LIBRARIES.

Towns and districts are both authorized to maintain school libraries and a slight annual expenditure added to the State aid for the supply of school apparatus, would soon suffice to equip every school with a good working library, than which no better educational power exists. In towns where there is no public library and where the population is so scattered as to preclude the maintenance of one central library, such school libraries should be established without fail and maintained at a high degree of efficiency.

In addition to these school libraries, towns are authorized to establish and maintain free public libraries, and several of the towns have such libraries already established. In a large number of other towns there are free libraries, but they are controlled by associations, either chartered directly by the General Assembly, or organized under the general law relating to "Voluntary Associations." The State Board of

Education is authorized to grant aid from the State treasury to all such free public libraries. The main condition is that the use of the library shall be entirely free to all the citizens, subject only to such rules as are necessary for the proper care of the property. This aid cannot be given until the library has attained to the size of five hundred volumes. The amount of aid is fifty dollars annually for the first five hundred volumes, and twenty-five dollars additional for each subsequent five hundred. This increase is, however, optional with the Board of Education. The Board are authorized to make rules and regulations for the government of these libraries. Copies of these rules can be had always on application to the commissioner.

If possible it is desirable to establish these libraries upon a permanent basis, and that is best secured by making them town institutions. Provision is thereby made for their constant care and protection and the general public is more thoroughly interested in them. It often happens however that the first inception of such an enterprise must be in the minds of a few public spirited persons, and in that case they should associate themselves together. An outline of the necessary articles for such an association will be found among the "Forms."

COURSE OF STUDIES.

The following Course of Studies has been prepared mainly for the ungraded, or district, schools. It is believed, however, that it will be found adapted, in its general outlines, to any system of graded schools. It is therefore commended to all schools that are working without any definite plan.

FIRST YEAR.

Reading. The word or sentence method is recommended for beginners as preferable to the alphabet method alone. Free use should be made of the blackboard. By means of it the whole class may be taught as successfully as a single pupil. Be cautious in teaching words before the pupils possess the ideas which they are designed to represent. The work of this year should be that usually covered by any First Reader.

Spelling. At first depend entirely upon the copying by the pupils of the words on the blackboard and selections from the reader. Use only the script form of letters. As fast as the pupils acquire a knowledge of the names of the letters, oral spelling can be introduced as a change.

Numbers. Teach numbers from 1 to 10; using first various objects, then giving the names and also the figures. Teach with each number all the possible combinations in addition, subtraction, multiplication and division.

Vocal Music. Begin with G for 1, and teach the first five tones of the scale, using syllables, scale names and words. Secure good articulation and quality of tone. Practice writing the notes in various combinations. Teach simple, but pleasing *rote* songs. Vocal exercises.

Drawing. Teach ideas of measure, points and lines; names of lines drawn in different directions and angles, with the names of the different kinds.

Manners and Morals. Give attention to habits of personal cleanliness. Present and enforce moral truths by means of anecdote and illustration.

SECOND YEAR.

Reading. Second Reader begun. Other reading of the same grade. Awaken the ideas in the pupil's mind, before he attempts to express them. Teach the names and common uses of the punctuation marks.

Spelling. Make up the exercises mainly from the reading lessons and from words representing familiar objects. The work should be mainly in writing.

Penmanship. Begin formal and systematic instruction. Use slates ruled for the purpose, or paper with lead pencil. Begin with the letters

i—u—e—m—n—l—t

At first do not be too critical. Aim at a general uniformity in size and slope. Tracing books may be used here and in the next grade to assist in the work.

Numbers. Teach the different numbers up to 20, as in the case of the first ten. Teach also the writing and reading of numbers up to 100. Begin combinations of operations with small numbers, as addition with multiplication, or subtraction with division. Aim at great facility and accuracy in the use of the first twenty numbers. Teach the Roman notation only as far as you have gone with the Arabic.

Language. Begin to teach the *use* of language by first talking with children about familiar objects. These exercises should always be carefully prepared beforehand, and should be so arranged as, first, to lead the pupils to think and speak for themselves, and second, to leave distinct and proper impressions on their minds. Having obtained oral statements, or descriptions from the pupils, then require them to write out the same thing on slate or paper. Be satisfied with short and easy steps at first.

Vocal Music. Carry forward the work in the same manner as in first year, up to (6) E. Practice on the intervals 1—3, 3—5, 2—4. Pay special attention to the tone, that it does not become loud and harsh. Rote songs as before.

Drawing. Teach the different geometrical forms involving straight lines. Simple dictation exercises introducing design.

Manners and Morals. General behavior in the relations of pupils with one another, with their parents, and with their elders or superiors. Enforce this and all the moral virtues by precept, example and illustration, daily.

THIRD YEAR.

Reading. Second Reader completed, and other reading matter of similar grade. Begin teaching the simplest form of analysis of the reading lesson, thus preparing the pupil for a proper *study* of his lesson.

Spelling. Depend chiefly upon the written exercises, looking out for accuracy and neatness of execution. The spelling-book proper may be introduced with care that too difficult words are not taken.

Penmanship. Teach the rest of the letters of the alphabet. Watch the pupils carefully for the detection of radical errors and wrong tendencies, and aim especially for the correction of the same.

Numbers. Write numbers up to 1000. Teach the principles of the decimal method of numeration. Make applications with United States money, and measures of length and capacity, both common and metric.

Language. Exercises as in the previous year, increasing gradually their scope and fulness. Call for the products of the memory, either what they may have read or heard. Teach the use of capitals and the period.

Geography. Preparatory work. Begin with lessons on form, size and place. Teach the structure and use of a map or plan. Teach the various geographical terms, such as surface, hill, plain, source, shore, etc., as far as possible from the objects themselves, and in their absence, from drawings or illustrations.

Vocal Music. Begin to teach simple songs by note, key of C. Complete the work of mastering the scale, using any tone from C to F for 1. Teach right use of note, scale, staff and names of degrees of the staff.

Drawing. Curved lines and geometrical forms involving them. Secure as accurate work as possible. Begin object drawing. Original design.

Manners and Morals. General behavior in public places. Seek for and improve every opportunity to inculcate the highest type of morality.

FOURTH YEAR.

Reading. Third Reader and other matter of the same grade. Continue analysis of the reading lesson. Begin to note minor matters in enunciation, pronunciation, etc., and secure their correction. Avoid all concert reading, except in case of short selections for drill purposes.

Spelling. Continue as before. See that all *new* words in the reading lessons are learned.

Penmanship. Begin with regular copy books. Practice freely on waste paper. Let the *teaching* be mainly done to *all* of the pupils at the same time. Dwell upon the formation of the several letters, securing perfect concert of action.

Arithmetic. Begin written arithmetic. Carry notation and numeration to billions. Go through the fundamental operations, deriving all rules from the processes. Aim for and *secure* facility and accuracy.

Language. Have the pupils write out analysis of the reading lesson. Let them write short accounts of familiar objects or scenes. Scan the exercises as carefully for that which is praiseworthy, as for the errors. Be judicious in your criticisms.

Geography. Teach the earth as a whole from the globe, its form, size, motion, etc.; its grand divisions, and main features. Construct map of the hemispheres.

Vocal Music. Continue work of the third grade, letting any degree of the staff represent the pitch 1. Pure, sweet tones to be studiously sought for, not only in these exercises, but also in the recitations. Reading at sight, key of C.

Drawing. Free hand from flat copies. Dictation exercises by the teacher. Drawing from memory. Original design.

Manners and Morals. Carry out the plan as set forth in the preceding years, endeavoring always to leave a vivid and definite impression upon the pupil's mind.

FIFTH YEAR.

Reading. Third Reader completed, and matter of similar grade. Memorizing of choice selections. Let the reading lesson include thorough knowledge of the persons, places and events connected therewith.

Spelling. Continue the same plan as last year, keeping the classes of words to be learned within the ready mastery and comprehension of the pupils.

Penmanship. Two numbers in the copy-books. Drill the whole school as before in the proper movements of the fingers and forearm.

Arithmetic. Review from the beginning *thoroughly* through division, paying attention only to the *simple* operations. Give practical problems for solution. Make the pupils obtain material or data for problems of their own. Require explanation or reasoning only so far as the pupil can understand it. Avoid all mere repetitions of formulas of words.

Geography. Begin with the western continent. Teach its divisions. Then take the United States as a whole, and teach its subdivisions; then the New England States and lastly Rhode Island in detail. Have the pupils draw maps of all countries or localities studied.

Vocal Music. Review of preceding topics, with definitions. Teach relative and absolute pitch.

Drawing. Free-hand from memory. Free-hand from flat copies. Dictation exercises. Original design.

General Exercises. Elementary lessons on the *facts* of Botany and Mineralogy. Have pupils make collections. Manners and Morals enforced as before by anecdote, precept and example.

SIXTH YEAR.

Reading. Fourth Reader begun, with analyses.

Spelling. Special attention to syllabication. Look out for all geographical, historical and biographical names which occur in the other studies.

Penmanship. Two numbers of the copy-books. Carry on systematic *drill* for a short time each day.

Arithmetic. Through fractions, common and decimal. Finish the Metric System. Take examples and problems from daily life.

Language. Grammatical forms, and simple analysis. Frequent written exercises. Let each be brief, but for a specific purpose.

Geography. Complete the United States and the rest of North America.

Vocal Music. Daily practice in reading simple music written in the scale of C and G. Teach two-part songs by note. Practice in semi-tones.

Drawing. Continue same course as last year, with addition of object drawing and of models from flat copy.

General Exercises. Exercises in Zoology, with those birds and animals which can be obtained, or which are familiar to the pupils. Manners and Morals to be strictly conserved.

SEVENTH YEAR.

Reading. Fourth Reader concluded, and reading matter from various sources. Recitations of selections. Require careful study of the lesson, for the *thought*, and secure the corresponding proper expression.

Spelling. Continue as in preceding year.

Penmanship. Two numbers of the copy-books, with the regular drill exercises.

Arithmetic. Compound Numbers and Percentage. Let examples be such as shall give the pupils *facility* in their work.

Language. Continue analysis. Take up the simpler rules of syntax. Note and explain false syntax as it is found in the compositions or in conversation. Teach the work of making out a plan for a composition.

Geography. South America and Europe. Follow the principle of giving less and less detail, the farther the country is from the United States, or the less important it may be.

Vocal Music. Teach interval; compound intervals in the scale, and their names; intermediate tones, transpositions of the scale, and to read in the scales of G, D, A and E.

Drawing. Teach the principles of design. Freehand and memory work continued.

General Exercises. Lessons on the human body, with special reference to care of health. Manners and Morals in relation to health.

EIGHTH YEAR.

Reading. Fifth Reader. Outside selections. Work up all references in the reading lesson, which would throw light upon it.

Spelling. Frequent reviews of the work of the earlier years should be interspersed in the regular lessons. Continue the spelling of all technical words which occur in the regular studies.

Penmanship. Business forms, bills, letters, etc.

Arithmetic. Interest, simple and compound, with all of the common applications of both percentage and interest.

Language. Continue analysis and work in syntax. Increase the scope of the compositions. Begin to correct and explain the simpler rhetorical errors.

Geography. Asia and Africa.

History. United States History, by topics, as far as time or circumstances will allow.

Vocal Music. Review work of previous year. Teach the scales of D, A and E, and first and second transposition by flats. Practice reading in any scale already taught, naming by letters or syllables, any intermediate tone that may be introduced.

Drawing. Same as last year.

General Exercises. Simple lessons in the elements of Natural Philosophy. Manners and Morals not to be overlooked.

NINTH YEAR.

Reading. Fifth Reader completed. Selections from the best authors.

Spelling. General review, both oral and written.

Arithmetic. Review from the beginning. Square and cube root, mensuration and such other advance topics as may be desired, or as time may permit.

Book-Keeping. The fundamental principles of debt and credit. Simple forms of accounts for ordinary purposes. Business details and other matters connected therewith.

Language. Critical study of good authors, both for grammatical matter, and also for rhetorical points. Composition continued, special care being given to *all* subjects *previously* taught.

Geography. The main features of physical geography. Show particularly effect of climate, etc., upon productions and the forms of animal life.

History. United States History concluded, with as much local history as time permits.

Vocal Music. Reviews. Teach scales of E flat and A flat. Sing two and three part songs. Pay special attention to those singing the lower part.

Drawing. Free-hand exercises, with design. Geometrical drawing.

General Exercises. Lessons in Natural Philosophy or Elementary Chemistry. Manners and Morals kept prominently before the pupils.

Suggestions. In the introduction of this scheme into any school, care must be taken that only so much be attempted as the *present* condition of the school demands. While the work is laid out by years, it should be kept in mind that the *order* of the topics is of primary importance. It may be necessary to increase or diminish the *length of time*, but the line of progression should be rigidly followed.

The "course" has been made more full than perhaps the majority of schools would at present demand, or the teachers be prepared to carry into practice. It is hoped, however, that it is not too high an ideal for any to strive for. At first such studies can be selected as are demanded, or are within the mastery of the teachers; leaving the others to be introduced as opportunity shall offer. Success in the introduction of this, or any course of studies, will depend upon the attention which is given to the work of the schools by the superintendent and committee. It will not run itself any better than any other machine. It must be guided.

FORMS.

These forms have been prepared in order to assist those who may be disposed to undertake any office or duty under the school laws, to save them expense and trouble, and to bring about a uniformity of practice, as far as can be done. These forms, with the exception of the oath of office, are not prescribed by law, but are believed to conform substantially to the law, and to be safe precedents.

1. *Warrant or Certificate of Election of School Officers.*

To of greeting:

This certifies that you, the said were at a [town or district] meeting, held on the day of A. D. 18 chosen to the office of of [the town or district No.] and are by virtue of said appointment fully authorized and empowered to discharge all the duties of said office, and to exercise all the powers thereto belonging, according to law.

[L. S.] Witness my hand, and the seal of said [town or district] hereto affixed by me, this day of A. D. 18 .

2. *Form of Oath to be taken by all School Officers.*

I, [naming the person] do solemnly swear (or affirm) that I will faithfully and impartially discharge the duties of the office of [naming the office] according to the best of my abilities, and that I will support the constitution and laws of this State and the constitution of the United States, so help me God; (or, this affirmation I make and give upon the peril of the penalty of perjury) according to Chap. 23, Sect 4, Public Statutes.

---

3. *Certificate of Engagement of School Officers.*

Town of A. D. 18

Before the subscriber personally appeared and took an oath to support the constitution of the United States, the constitution and laws of this State, and faithfully to discharge the duties of the office of school committee [or clerk, trustee, treasurer of school district No. , as the case may be] so long as he continues therein.

A. B., Justice of the Peace,
or Notary, as the case may be.

---

4. *Certificate to a Teacher from a Committee.*

This certifies that has passed a satisfactory examination in the branches required to be taught, and has given evidence of good moral character, and authority is hereby given to teach the department in the public schools in district No. of this town for from date unless this certificate is sooner annulled.

Town.

Date.

Chairman.
Clerk.
Supt.

NOTE. The above need not be signed by more than one of the officers designated.

---

5. *Form for Annulling a Certificate.*

To the trustees of school districts in the town of
and all others it may concern:

Whereas, the school committee of this town did, on the day of A. D. 18 issue to of a certificate of qualification as a teacher in the public schools: Now, know ye, that upon further examination, investigation and trial, the said has been found deficient and unqualified [or the said has refused to conform to the regulations made by the committee, as the case may be], and we do, therefore, by the authority given us by law, declare the said certificate to be annulled and void from this date, of which all persons whose duty it is to employ teachers of public schools, are hereby requested to take notice.

By order and in behalf of the school committee of the town of

Date. Chairman or Clerk.

NOTE. If a complaint is made against a teacher, it will be imperative that he shall be notified for at least five days before a decision on his case. And notice of the annulling should be immediately given to the trustees of the district, and generally, in order to prevent his being again employed.

6. *Memorandum of a Contract with a Teacher.*

This agreement, made this day of A. D. 18 between A. B., etc. [trustee, school committee or agent appointed by the school committee, as the case may be], of on the one part, and X. Y., of on the other part, witnesses, that the said X. Y. hereby agrees to teach, for the compensation herein mentioned, the school in and for said district or town, at [specify the building, if desired], for the term of months [or weeks] commencing and ending and the said X. Y. further engages to exert the utmost of his ability in conducting said school, and improving the education and morals of the scholars; to keep such registers and make such returns to the trustees and to the school committee as may be required of him, and in all respects to conform to all such regulations for the government of said school as may be made by the school committee of said town, and to the provisions of the laws regulating public schools. And in case the certificate of qualification of said X. Y. should be annulled, or if he shall not keep the register and make return, as aforesaid, or should violate such regulations as aforesaid, this agreement from thenceforth shall be of no effect. And the said [committee, trustee or agent] agree to pay the said X. Y. therefor at the rate of per month [or per week], to be paid at the end of each month [or the term] out of the school money by law apportioned to said district, and the legal assessments which may be made, and in no event out of the private property of the contractor. And it is further agreed, that the possession of the school-house and its appurtenances shall at all times be considered as being in the trustees [or school committee or superintendent].

[L. S.] Witness our hands and seals hereto, the day first above mentioned.

Sealed and executed
in presence of

---

7. Notice of a Meeting of a District called by the School Committee.

Notice is hereby given that there will be a meeting of the legal voters of school district No. in the town of at the school-house in said district [if no school-house, then the school committee must appoint a place], at o'clock in the noon, on the day of A. D. 18 for the purpose of organizing said district, of electing officers for said district for the ensuing year, of considering the expediency of building [or repairing] the school-house in said district, and laying a tax on the ratable property of the district therefor, and of transacting any other business which may lawfully come before said meeting.

By order and in behalf of the school committee of said town.

Date. Chairman, or Clerk.

---

8. Notice of Annual District Meeting.

To the legal voters of school district No. of the

town of the annual meeting of for the choice of officers and the transaction of any other business which may lawfully come before it, will be held at on the day of A. D. 18 at o'clock in the noon.

Date.

Trustee or Trustees.

---

9. *Notice of Special Meeting.*

A *special meeting* of the legal voters of school district No. in the town of will be held at the district school-house, on the day of A. D. 18 at o'clock [P. M.], for the purpose of [here insert every object that is to be brought before the meeting].

(Signed) A. B., Trustee.

NOTE. All notices of district meetings must be posted in two or more public places, or published in some newspaper, for at least five days before the meeting. That is, a notice for a meeting on a Saturday must be posted the preceding Monday. If called by the trustees at the request of five qualified voters, the notice must be posted within two days from the time the request was made. Care should always be taken to preserve evidence of the proper notification of the meeting. Every notice should be dated, and signed only by the committee or trustees.

---

10. *Form of Request to be made by five Legal Voters of a District to the District Trustees for the calling of a Special Meeting.*

To the District Trustees of School District No.

The undersigned, legal voters of school district No. of the town of request you, in pursuance of the school law, to call a special meeting of said district, for the purpose of

Dated this day of A. D. 18

(Signed)

---

11. *Commencement of District Records.*

For first meeting. At a meeting of the legal voters of school district No. of the town of called by the school committee of said town, and notified according to law [here in some cases it may be advisable to state particularly how the notice was given], and held according to notice at the district school-house [or as the case may be], on the day of A. D. 18 at o'clock in the noon.

For annual meeting. At the annual meeting of the legal voters of school district No. of the town of notified by the trustees of said district according to law [in some cases specify as above], and held according to notice at the district school-house [or as may be], on the day of A. D. 18 at o'clock in the noon.

For special meeting. At a meeting of the legal voters of school district No. of the town of held (in pursuance of an application to the trustees) at on and which meeting was duly notified by the trustees as the law requires.

For adjourned meeting. At a meeting of the legal voters of school district No. of the town of held according to adjournment, at on

12. *Record of the Choice of Officers, etc.*

The following named persons were chosen to the offices set against their respective names, viz.:

C. D., Clerk, etc. A. B., Moderator.

Or, instead of the above, say—

Voted, that A. B., be appointed moderator of this meeting.

Voted, that C. D., be appointed clerk [or trustee, treasurer, etc.], of this district [in place of O. P., resigned, etc., if such be the case], to hold his office until the next annual meeting, and until his successor is appointed.

The clerk then, in presence of the meeting, took the oath in the form prescribed in chapter 23, section 4, of the Public Statutes, administered by E. F., Esq., moderator [or notary public, justice of the peace, or town clerk, as the case may be].

It was moved by A. B., and seconded by C. D., that and after discussion the question was put and the motion was rejected, or adopted.

---

13. *Vote of District to devolve care of School on School Committee.*

Voted, (if the school committee of this town consent thereto and accept thereof), that all the powers and duties of this district, and the trustees thereof, relating to keeping public schools in this district be, and they are hereby devolved on said school committee, until this district shall choose a new trustee or trustees, or shall otherwise legally direct.

NOTE. A copy of this vote, with a proper heading, "At a meeting of," etc., attested by the clerk, should be furnished to the committee.

---

14. *Vote of District to build School-house.*

Voted, that a school-house be erected at or upon for the use of the public schools in this district, and that be a committee to cause the same to be erected, the said committee first procuring the plans and specifications for the building, to be approved by the committee of the town, according to law, and that the said shall have full power, in the name and behalf of the district, to sign, seal and execute any contracts which may be necessary to carry out this vote, to superintend the execution of said contracts, and to do any other matter or thing which may be necessary to carry out this vote.

NOTE. The location, (unless before made), must be made by the school committee.

---

15. *Form of Contract to build School-house.*

Articles of agreement made and executed on the day of A. D. 18 between A. B., of on the one part, and School District No. of the town of county of State of on the other part.

The said A. B., for himself, his heirs, executors and administrators, doth hereby covenant and agree with the school district and their assigns, that he, the said A. B., his heirs, executors and administrators, for the considerations herein expressed, shall, and will, within the space of months from the date hereof, erect, build, and completely cover over and finish upon [here describe the lot], and upon such spot in said lot as said school district or their proper officers may direct, a house, out-buildings and fences, for the purpose of a district school-house and appendages, according to plans, elevation and specifications more particularly expressed in a schedule hereto attached and signed by said parties, and which is hereby made part and parcel of this agreement; and also shall and will perform and execute all the works mentioned in the said schedule, and in the manner therein mentioned, and within the time aforesaid; and also shall and will furnish and provide at his own charge, good and sufficient materials of the sorts and quality expressed in said schedule, and all such other materials as may be necessary for the erecting and fully completing the house, out-houses and fences aforesaid, according to the plans and specifications aforesaid.

And it is further agreed between said parties, that if the said A. B., his heirs, executors or administrators, shall not, within the space of time above mentioned, finish and complete all said works as aforesaid, then said school district, or their agent, may go on and complete said works, at the cost and charge of the said A. B., his heirs, executors and administrators, and may deduct the same from the compensation herein agreed to be paid for said buildings and works; and the said A. B., his heirs, executors and administrators, shall also be liable for any other damages incurred by said district by said failure, and shall also be liable to said district for any damages incurred by any other unreasonable delay in completing the works aforesaid.

And the said school district doth hereby covenant and agree with the said A. B., his heirs, executors, administrators and assigns, that upon the completion of said works as aforesaid, the said school district shall and will pay to the said A. B., his executors, administrators or assigns, on or before the day of A. D. 18 the sum of dollars, as full compensation for his services in building and completing said works.

And it is further agreed, that if said school district or their agents shall direct any more work to be done upon or around said buildings than is hereinbefore agreed, the said district shall pay the expense thereof, in addition to the compensation aforesaid. And if said district or their agents shall direct to omit or diminish any part of the work hereinbefore agreed to be done and expressed in said schedule, then there shall be deducted from said compensation, a reasonable sum, according to the proportion said work omitted may bear to the work herein first agreed to be done. And said district or their proper agents shall have a right to direct any additions or omissions as aforesaid, and the party of the other part shall be bound to comply with and perform the said directions.

[*Clause to refer to arbitration.*]

And lastly, it is hereby agreed between the parties aforesaid, that if any dispute shall happen between the said district or its agents, and the said A. B., his heirs, executors, administrators, or assigns, in relation to the buildings herein agreed to be erected, work to be done, the payment of the money, or concerning the value and expense of any work directed to be added or omitted as hereinbefore mentioned, or concerning any other matter or thing whatever, relating to the construction of this agreement, or the amount of any damages claimed by either party, under its provisions, or for any alleged violation thereof, then in such case such dispute shall, upon the demand of either party, be left to the award and determination of three indifferent persons, one to be appointed in writing by each of said parties, immediately thereafter, and a third to be appointed in writing by the two persons so first named. And the said parties hereby covenant and agree with each other, that they will severally abide by, perform and keep the award and determination of the said three persons, or any two of them, touching said disputes, provided said award be made under the hands and seals of said arbitrators or any two of them, within from the time of said reference.

In testimony whereof, the said A. B. hath hereto set his hand and seal, and said district, have hereto affixed their seal by the hands of duly authorized for that purpose, who hath [or have] hereto also set their own hands.

Names of committee or agents. [L. S.]

Sealed and delivered
in presence of [L. S.]

NOTE. If the district wishes a surety for the performance of a contract of A. B., it may be taken by a bond, conditioned for the performance by A. B. of the covenants and agreements in an instrument dated [and then briefly describe it.]

16. Record of a Vote of District to Tax.

At the annual meeting of the legal voters of school district No. of the town of held at on according to legal notice issued and signed by and posted up at for the five days previous required by law [or, at a special meeting of, etc., called by, etc.]

Whereas, this district has voted to build a school-house in and for said district [or, to repair the district school-house, whatever the cause may be],

Voted, that for the purpose of defraying the expense thereof, a tax of the sum of dollars [or of cents on the hundred dollars] be assessed upon, levied and collected from the ratable property in this district, in manner provided by law, [and according to the estimate, apportionment and value which shall be affixed to said ratable estates in the assessment and tax bill of this town which shall next be completed after the date of this vote].

NOTE. The above form is a proper one to submit to the committee for their approval. It should be signed by the clerk of the district.

In case nothing is said about valuation, the law directs the tax to be assessed on the last previous town valuation. If, however, the district wishes it assessed on the next valuation, it can be done by including the last clause.

Cautions for District Meetings about to assess a tax.

If there is any doubt about the boundaries of the district, have them defined by the committee.

Have the meeting notified for the proper length of time, the notices put up as required, and, if the meeting is a special one, let the notice express clearly the object of the meeting, and evidence of the notice should be preserved.

See that only tax-payers vote on the proposition.

Have all the officers properly engaged. Specify the amount or rate of tax, and when to be collected.

The district may give the collection to the regular collector, if there be one, or, if there be none, may appoint a collector, or may vote to have it collected by the town collector.

The district need not, but may, require bonds of the collector or treasurer; if they do they should fix the sum and approve the sureties.

They should agree with the collector for his fees, otherwise he will be entitled to five per cent.

They may offer a deduction to those who pay on or before a specified time, and may impose a percentage on those who do not pay until after such time.

The location of the house, the plan of the house or repairs, and the amount of the tax, must all be approved by the school committee, if not already done.

---

17. *Form of a Tax Bill.*

Assessment of the taxes upon the ratable estates in school district No. of the town of made by the trustees thereof, according to law, this day of A. D. 18 for the purpose of raising the sum of dollars, according to a vote of said district, passed on the day of A. D. 18

Names.	Real.	Personal.	Total.	Tax.

NOTE. The trustees must sign the tax bill. If the town assessors are applied to, it would be well to have them make their certificate at the foot of the tax bill, and sign it. The real and personal lists must be kept separate.

---

18. *Warrant to Collect a Tax,*

To A. B., collector of taxes of school district No. of the town of county of and State of Rhode Island and Providence Plantations:—

GREETING

You, having been appointed collector of taxes for said district, are hereby, in the name of said State, authorized and required to proceed and collect the tax specified in the annexed rate bill, according to law, and to pay the same to the treasurer of the district, or to his successor in office, and for so doing this shall be your sufficient warrant.

Given under my hand and seal, at this day of A. D. 18

C. D. [L. S.]

Trustee of said school district.

NOTE. The trustee must issue and sign this warrant in addition to the tax bill as above. The collector should also receive from the district clerk a warrant or formal certificate of election, which may be in substance according to the form No. 1, and then his engagement can be certified upon the back.

If a bond is required the district should approve the sum and sureties of the bond, and the clerk should certify the fact thereon.

If the town collector is appointed to collect the tax, the above will need to be changed in the first line by striking out the words "of school district No. " and in the fourth line by striking out the words "for said district" and inserting the words "by school district No. of said town."

---

19. District Treasurer's Bond.

Know all men, that we, A. B., of county of and State of Rhode Island and Providence Plantations, as principal, and C. D., of county of and State aforesaid, as surety [or sureties to the satisfaction of the district], are firmly held and bound unto the school district No. of the town of and State aforesaid, in the full sum of [to be fixed by the district] to be paid to the said school district or their assigns, to which we hereby jointly and severally bind ourselves, our several and respective heirs, executors and administrators.

Sealed and dated the day of A. D. 18

The condition of the foregoing obligation is, that whereas the said A. B. was, at a meeting of said school district, holden , appointed treasurer of said district. Now, if he shall faithfully discharge the duties of said office during his continuance therein, and at the expiration of his office, he or his executors or administrators shall exhibit a true account, if required, and deliver over to his successor, or the order of the district, all books, papers and moneys belonging to the district, in his hands, then the above obligation is to be void, otherwise to remain in force.

Executed in presence of

.... [L. S.]

[L. S.]

NOTE. It may be advisable for the treasurer to receive a formal certificate of appointment, or warrant, and then his engagement can be endorsed upon it. The above bond need not be given unless the district require it.

---

20. District Collector's Bond.

Know all men, that we, A. B., of State of Rhode Island and Providence Plantations, as principal, and C. D., of as surety, are firmly held and bound unto E. F., of , treasurer of school district No. in the town of and State aforesaid, in the full sum of [to be fixed by the district, not exceeding double the tax] to be paid to said his successors in said office, or assigns, to which we jointly bind ourselves, our several and respective heirs, executors and administrators.

Sealed and dated this day of A. D. 18

The condition of this obligation is, that whereas the

said A. B. was, at a meeting of the legal voters of school district No. of the town of appointed collector of the rates and taxes assessed and to be assessed in, by, and upon said district, and the said A. B. has accepted said office ; and whereas said district on the day of A. D. 18 voted that a tax of be assessed on all the ratable property in said district, for the purpose of and said tax has been legally assessed, and the trustee of said district hath issued his warrant to said collector, with said rate bill annexed, for the collection of said tax, the receipt of which said rate bill and warrant is hereby acknowledged, and by which said warrant said tax is to be collected and paid over, on or before the day of A. D. 18 Now if the said A. B. shall faithfully perform and discharge said office and trust, and with diligence and fidelity levy and collect, as far as may be done, all the taxes that have been, or may be so committed to him for collection, during his continuance in office, and he, his heirs, executors or administrators shall, at all times on proper demand, render an account and pay over all the proceeds of such collections to the treasurer of said district, or his successors in office, according to the directions contained in the warrants for their collection, then this obligation is to be void, otherwise to remain in force.

Executed in presence of

.... [L. S.]

.... [L. S.]

NOTE. The district collector need not give bond, unless required, but the law requires the town collector to give a bond satisfactory to the school committee. The above form can be readily changed so as to render it suitable in case of the town collector.

21. *Form of Tax Collector's Deed.*

To all to whom these presents may come. I, A. B., of county of and State of Rhode Island and Providence Plantations, collector of taxes of school district No. in said town, send greeting :—

Whereas the said school district, at a meeting duly notified, and held on the day of A. D. 18 voted that a tax of dollars be assessed on the ratable property in said district, for the purpose of and said tax was afterwards, viz. : on the day of A. D. 18 assessed according to law, and the tax bill in due form delivered to me the said collector, with a warrant attached thereto, signed by the trustees of said district, requiring me to proceed according to law and collect the said tax, and pay over the same to the treasurer of the district, or to his successor in office, and whereas C. D., of neglected to pay the tax assessed against him, and expressed in the said tax bill, amounting to the sum of dollars, and in consequence thereof, I did on the day of levy said warrant upon a certain lot or tract of land belonging to said C. D., in said district, and did advertise the same for sale according to law, at two [or more] public places in said town, for twenty days previous to sale [and also in the newspaper printed in], and on the day of A. D. 18 at o'clock in the noon, on the premises, being the time and place appointed, I proceeded to sell at auction so much of said land as was necessary to satisfy said tax and the incidental expenses, and E. F., of was the highest bidder therefor.

Now, know ye, that in consideration of the sum of dollars, being the amount of said tax and expenses paid me by the said E. F., I, the said collector, do hereby give, grant, bargain, sell and convey unto the said E. F., his heirs and assigns, all the right, title and interest which said C. D. had at the time of assessing said tax, in and to the following described tract of land, situated in the district and town aforesaid, containing acres [more or less], and bounded [describe], or however otherwise bounded, with all [buildings] and appurtenances, being so much of said land of the said C. D., levied on as was necessary to satisfy said tax and expenses; to have and to hold the same to said E. F., his heirs and assigns forever, subject to the right of redemption provided by law. And I, the said A. B., for myself, my heirs, executors and administrators, do covenant with said E. F., his heirs and assigns, that I [have given bond and] have advertised said property as hereinbefore stated, and have complied with the terms of the law regulating the collecting of taxes, in respect to said sale, as hereinbefore stated.

Witness my hand and seal, this day of A. D. 18

A. B. [L. S.]

Signed, sealed and delivered
in presence of

Town of, etc., A. D. 18 Before me the subscriber, appeared A. B., collector of taxes of school district No. of the town of and acknowledged the foregoing to be his free act and deed, and his hand and seal to be thereunto affixed.

O. P.

Justice of the Peace, Notary Public or Town Clerk.

NOTE. In case where town collector acts, the only change in the above will be in the third line, by dropping the words "of school district No." In case of unimproved lands owned by persons out of the State, and also of improved lands when neither the owner nor occupant lives in the State, notice of the sale must be given twenty days in a newspaper. The purchaser under a tax collector's deed should see that the law has been complied with, and that his evidence of advertising is preserved.

---

22. *Form of a Lease.*

These articles of agreement made this day of A. D. 18 witness that A. B., of doth hereby demise and let unto the school district No. of the town of [describe the room or building] with the appurtenances, in consideration of the rents and covenants by said school district herein mentioned to be performed, to have and hold the same to the said school district and their assigns for the space of year, commencing on the day of A. D. 18 and ending on the day of A. D. 18 for the purpose of keeping a district school therein, and holding such schools or lectures or other literary meetings, or meetings of business, as the school committee or the officers of said district may deem advisable for promoting the cause of education. And the said district agrees to pay therefor the sum of per annum as rent, and at that rate for any less time than a year, the payment to be made to the said A.

B., his heirs or assigns, at his residence, on the last day of the year [or on the last day of each year in the term], without any notice or demand therefor [provisions about repairs, loss by fire, etc., may be here inserted].

Witness the hand and seal of said A. B., and the seal of the said district hereto affixed by by said district duly authorized, the day and year first above mentioned.

Sealed and executed
in presence of

[L. S.]

[L. S.]

---

23. *Vote to take a Lease.*

The district may authorize a person to execute a lease for them by a vote as follows:

" *Voted*, that the trustees of the district [or treasurer] be and they are hereby fully empowered to hire a building for the purposes of a school-house for the district [here specify the building, and fix the time and conditions or leave them at discretion], and to make and execute the necessary contracts therefor, and to seal, deliver and acknowledge the same in the name and behalf of the district.

NOTE. If the above lease is to be acknowledged, see the form of acknowledgment to No. 26.

A certified copy of the above vote should be given by the district clerk to the person authorized to take the lease.

24. *Deed to a School District.*

Know all men, that I, A. B. of in the State of Rhode Island and Providence Plantations, in consideration of the sum of paid me by C. D., treasurer of school district No. in the town of and State aforesaid, the receipt of which I acknowledge, and am therewith fully satisfied and paid [if a gift, say, in consideration of my desire to aid and assist in diffusing the benefits of a good common school education among the inhabitants of school district No. etc., as the grantor pleases] do hereby give, grant, enfeoff, convey and confirm unto said school district and their assigns, a certain lot of land situated in said town of [describe] or however otherwise bounded, with all the appurtenances and privileges thereto belonging, to have and to hold the same forever to said school district [and their assigns, but if there is a desire to prevent the lot ever being used for any other purpose, omit assigns and say, for the purpose of maintaining thereon a district schoolhouse and its appurtenances, for the benefit of the district school of said district, and for no other use or purpose whatever]. And I, the said A. B., do hereby for myself, my heirs, executors and administrators, covenant and engage to and with said school district [and their assigns] that the premises are free of all incumbrances, and I have good right to sell and convey as aforesaid, and that I, my heirs, executors and administrators shall and will for ever warrant, secure and defend the premises to said school district [and their assigns or to and for the purpose aforesaid], against the lawful claims of all persons whatsoever. And I, E. F., wife of the said A. B., for the consideration paid my said husband, hereby release unto said school district [and their assigns] all my right of dower in the premises. [If the premises are under mortgage, a release may be here inserted.] And I, G. H., of in consideration of the sum of paid to me by to my full satisfaction, do hereby give, grant, bargain, sell, assign and convey unto said school district [and their assigns], all the right, title and interest which I have in the premises by virtue of any mortgage deed thereof [or of any other claim or title whatsoever.] In witness whereof we have hereunto set our hands and seals this day of A. D. 18

.... [L. S.]

.... [L. S.]

.... [L. S.]

Signed, sealed and delivered
in presence of

State of county of town of A. D. 18 This day personally appeared before me and acknowledged the foregoing instrument to be voluntary act and deed and hand and seal to be thereunto affixed.

Before me, O. P., Justice of the Peace, Notary Public or Town Clerk (if executed in Rhode Island).

NOTE. If the land belongs to a married woman, her name should be inserted as one of the grantors, and the deed altered accordingly. She must acknowledge separately from her husband. Use the words of the law in the certificate of acknowledgment. See Public Statutes.

25. *Vote appointing an Attorney to sell land belonging to the District.*

At a meeting of the legal voters of school district No. of the town of etc., notified as the law requires, and held at on the day of A. D. 18

Voted, that A. B., treasurer of said school district, be and he is hereby appointed the agent and attorney of the district, to sell at his discretion, a certain lot of land, situated in and belonging to the district, containing bounded with the buildings and appurtenances, and with full power to affix the seal of the district to a deed or deeds conveying the same [with covenants of warranty or not, as the district may vote], and in the name of the district to acknowledge and deliver the same, and receive the purchase-money, and give a full discharge therefor.

A true copy of record: Witness,

E. F., Clerk of said District.

---

26. *District Land Deed.*

Know all men, that the school district No. of the town of county of State of Rhode Island and Providence Plantations, in consideration of the sum of paid to A. B., treasurer of said district, to and for the use of said district, by M. N., of the receipt of which is hereby acknowledged, does hereby give, grant, bargain, sell and convey unto the said M. N., his heirs and assigns, all the right, title and interest of said school district, in and to a lot of land situated in said district, containing bounded or however otherwise bounded, with all buildings and appurtenances, being the same lot conveyed to said district by deed of H. I. To have and to hold the same to said M. N., his heirs and assigns, forever. In testimony whereof, the said school district have hereunto fixed their seal, by the hands of said A. B., their treasurer, duly appointed for that purpose, at a legal meeting of said district, and the said treasurer hath hereunto affixed his own hand, this day of A. D. 18

A. B., Treasurer as aforesaid. [L. S.]

Signed and sealed in presence of

Acknowledgment.

State of Rhode Island and Providence Plantations, county of town of A. D. 18 The school district No. of said town, by A. B., their treasurer and attorney for that purpose, by vote of said district appointed, acknowledged the foregoing to be their voluntary act and deed, and their seal to be thereto affixed; and the said A. B., treasurer and attorney as aforesaid, also acknowledged his own hand affixed thereto, and that the same was the voluntary act and deed of himself and of the said district.

Before me,

P. Q.,

Justice of the Peace, or Notary Public, or Town Clerk.

NOTE. It will seldom, if ever, be advisable for a district to give anything more than a quit claim deed. If they wish to insert any warranty, it would be best to consult a well informed attorney.

27. *Vote to hire Money.*

Voted, that the treasurer of this school district be and hereby is authorized to hire dollars for the purpose of [here specify the uses to be made of the money] and to give the note of the district for the same.

NOTE. If any instructions as to rate of interest or time are to be given they should be inserted immediately after the word "dollars."

---

28. *District Note.*

$..................

.... R. I., ... 18

For value received School District No. of the town of of the county of and State of Rhode Island, promises to pay A. B., or order, dollars on demand [or if a time note, state the time], with interest, in accordance with the vote of said district, passed at a meeting held on the day of A. D. 18

C. D., Treasurer.

---

29. *Vote of District to establish a Secondary School.*

Voted, That this district will unite with school district No. of this town [or in the adjoining town of], in the establishment of a secondary school, according to the laws regulating public schools, for the common benefit of both said districts; provided said school district No. shall also give their consent thereto [within from this date], and that the clerk of the district furnish a certified copy of this vote to said school district No. and also to the school committee that [if said district consents] they may take the necessary measures for establishing said school.

---

30. Vote Prescribing Form of District Seal.

Voted, That the clerk of the district cause to be made a seal for the use of the district, with the figure of engraven thereon, and the letters or inscription around its margin, and that the same is hereby adopted, and declared to be the common seal of this corporation, and shall be kept by the clerk of the district.

NOTE. Every town, district, or other corporation, shall have a common seal, with a suitable device; but if they have no regular seal, any seal may be affixed to any instrument by their authority; for instance, a piece of paper attached by a wafer will be considered to be their seal.

---

31. Order on School Fund.

To treasurer of the town of

Pay to on account of school district No. of this town, or order, the sum of for

By order of the school committee of the town.

Chairman or Clerk.

Date.

NOTE. No order can legally be given on the town treasurer except in payment for services rendered or expenses actually incurred.

32. *Vote of School Committee to form Joint District.*

Voted, [the school committee of the town of concurring herewith] that a joint district be formed according to the provisions of the acts relating to public schools, to consist of school district No. of this town, and school district No. of said town of and that said districts shall constitute a joint district from the time that the school committee of said town of shall concur herewith [or if they have already passed a similar vote say, from and after the passage of this vote].

Voted further, that the chairman be authorized, in conjunction with the school committee of said town of to cause notices to be posted up [in one or more places in each of the two districts—specify them] for the first meeting of said joint district, to be held at on at o'clock in the noon [or to be held at such time and place as he may agree upon with the school committee of said town of] and that the clerk of the committee furnish a certified copy of this vote to the school committee of the said town of

NOTE. A notice signed by the chairman or clerk of each committee should be posted up in one or more places in each district. After trustees are elected, they will notify the subsequent meetings.

---

33. *Notice of Change in Text-Books.*

Notice is hereby given that a change in text-books in the study of will be proposed for consideration at the next regular meeting, [or at a meeting to be held on (here state the time)].

Signed,

NOTE. The above notice must be given at a *regular* meeting of the committee.

---

34. An Appeal.

To A. B., commissioner of public schools of the State of Rhode Island and Providence Plantations:

Whereas, the school committee, [trustees of school district No. of the town of No.], did at a meeting on the day of A. D. 18 pass a vote—[here copy or insert the substance, as nearly as can be procured]. I, the subscriber, according to law, do hereby appeal to you from said vote or decision, and claim that the same may be reversed. [Here state plainly and briefly the reasons].

Signed,

---

35. Notice of Appeal.

To the School Committee of the town of [trustees of school district No. in the town of]

I hereby notify you, that in conformity with the provisions of the laws regulating public schools, I appeal to A. B., commissioner of public schools, from [here specify the vote or decision of the committee, trustees, or district, which is complained of].

Signed,

Date. C. D.

A copy of this notice should be immediately served upon the clerk of the committee, clerk of the district, or upon the trustee, or trustees who have done the act complained of, or upon the parties interested, whoever they may be. In general it is full as well to send a copy of the appeal to the parties. It generally tends to expedite the matter.

---

36. *Form of Incorporation for a Public Library.*

The following is submitted as a suitable form for the constitution of an association for establishing and maintaining a free public library:

We, the subscribers, agree to associate and incorporate ourselves for the purpose of maintaining a public library, by the name of the under the provisions contained for that purpose in chapter 160 of the Public Statutes, and to be governed by the following constitution:

ARTICLE 1. This association shall be called the The library shall be established and maintained at in the town of

2. The officers of the association shall be a president, vice-president, secretary, treasurer, and librarian, who shall constitute a board of directors for the management of the business of the association, according to such rules as the association may from time to time adopt.

3. The annual meeting shall be held at on when the above-named officers shall be elected. Any

officer shall be elected by ballot if demanded by any members. Special meetings may be held at any time upon the call of the president or secretary, public notice having been given at least five days before holding the meeting.

4. Any member, for disorderly or immoral conduct, may be expelled, and any officer, for misconduct, may be removed at any regularly notified meeting of the society.

5. The directors may make all such regulations as they may deem proper for the government of the library, and prescribe fines for non-compliance, and may, in any case of misuse of books, prohibit any person from using the library until satisfaction is made.

6. The library shall be held by the association, not in shares for the benefit of shareholders, but in trust for the public benefit; to be open to all who shall comply with such reasonable rules as shall from time to time be made by the association or directors; and for the purpose of continuing the existence of the corporation, the association will from time to time elect as members such persons as they shall think most likely to co-operate zealously in promoting its objects. No member shall be admitted unless proposed at a previous meeting.

7. This constitution may be amended at any annual meeting, provided notice of the intended amendment has been given at some previous meeting. The secretary shall cause this constitution and all alterations thereof to be recorded in the records of land evidence of the town of as the law requires.

The above are all the provisions necessary to be inserted in the constitution. All other provisions are better made in the shape of rules or regulations, which may be altered from time to time with less trouble.

Whenever it is intended to establish a permanent library, it will always be most prudent to be incorporated as above. If a library is owned by several persons unincorporated, it will be liable to division, and each one's interest liable to attachment. In a corporation, the share only could be attached, and where the corporation hold the library merely as trustees (as provided in Art. 6, above), no individual would have any attachable interest whatever.

---

37. *Forms of Prayer.*

BEFORE ENTERING UPON THE WORK OF THE DAY.

O Lord our heavenly Father, Almighty and Everlasting God, who hath safely brought us to the beginning of this day, defend us in the same by Thy mighty power; and grant that this day we fall into no sin, neither run into any kind of danger, but that all our doings may be ordered of Thee to do always that which is righteous in Thy sight, through Jesus Christ our Lord. Amen.

O Almighty God, the giver of every good and perfect gift, the fountain of all wisdom, enlighten, we beseech Thee, our understandings by Thy Holy Spirit, and grant that whilst with all diligence and sincerity we apply ourselves to the attainment of human knowledge, we fail not constantly to strive after that wisdom which makes wise unto salvation; that so, through Thy mercy, we may daily be advanced both in learning and godliness, to the honor and praise of Thy name, through Jesus Christ our Lord. Amen.

Our Father which art in heaven, hallowed be Thy name, Thy kingdom come, Thy will be done in earth as it is in heaven; give us this day our daily bread; and forgive us our trespasses as we forgive them that trespass against us; and lead us not into temptation, but deliver us from evil; for Thine is the kingdom, the power and the glory, for ever and ever. Amen.

AT THE CLOSE OF THE WORK OF THE DAY.

Most merciful God, we yield Thee our humble and hearty thanks for Thy fatherly care and preservation of us this day, and for the progress which Thou hast enabled us to make in useful learning: We pray Thee to impress upon our minds whatever good instructions we have received, and to bless them to the advancement of our temporal and eternal welfare; and pardon, we implore Thee, all that Thou hast seen amiss in our thoughts, words and actions. May Thy good providence still guide and keep us during the approaching interval of rest and relaxation, so that we may be thereby prepared to enter on the duties of the morrow with renewed vigor, both of body and mind; and preserve us, we beseech Thee, now and ever, both outwardly in our bodies, and inwardly in our souls, for the sake of Jesus Christ, Thy Son, our Lord. Amen.

Lighten our darkness, we beseech Thee, O Lord; and by thy great mercy, defend us from all perils and dangers of this night, for the love of Thine only Son, our Saviour, Jesus Christ. Amen.

INDEX TO PUBLIC STATUTES.

[a. stands for article; con. for constitution; c. for chapter; s. for section, and p. for page.]

Index to Decisions, Remarks and Forms.

PUBLIC LAWS.

JANUARY SESSION, 1883.

CHAPTER 363.

ACT IN RELATION TO TRUANT CHILDREN, AND OF THE ATTENDANCE OF CHILDREN IN THE PUBLIC SCHOOLS.

enacted by the General Assembly as follows:

Section 1. Every person having under his control a hild between the ages of seven and fifteen years shall nnually cause such child to attend, for at least twelve weeks, six at least of which shall be consecutive, some public day school in the town in which such child resides; and for every neglect of such duty, the person so offending shall be fined not exceeding twenty dollars; but if such child shall have attended for a like period of time a private day school approved by the school committee of such town, or if such child shall have been otherwise furnished for a like period of time with the means of education, or shall have already acquired the elementary branches of learning taught in the public schools, or if his physical or mental condition was such as to render such attendance inexpedient or impracticable, then such penalty shall not be incurred.

SEC. 2. For the purposes of the preceding section school committees shall approve a private school only when the teaching therein is in the English language, and when they are satisfied that such teaching is thorough and efficient, but they shall not refuse to approve a private school on account of the religious teaching therein.

SEC. 3. The town council of each town and the city council of each city shall annually appoint one or more special constables, and fix their compensation, who shall be truant officers, and who shall, under the direction of the school committee, inquire into all cases arising under the provisions of this act, or under any ordinances made in pursuance thereof by the town by which such officers were appointed, and shall alone be authorized, in case of violation thereof, to make complaint therefor; they shall also serve all legal processes issued in pursuance of this act, but shall not be entitled to receive any fees for such service.

SEC. 4. The truant officers and the school committees of the several towns shall inquire into all cases of neglect of the duty prescribed in section 1 of this act within their respective towns, and ascertain the reasons, if any, therefor; and such truant officers, or any of them, shall, when so directed by the school committee, prosecute any person liable to the penalty provided for in said section 1.

SEC. 5. No child under ten years of age shall be employed in any manufacturing or mechanical establishment in this state; and any parent or guardian who permits such employment shall for every such offence be fined not exceeding twenty dollars.

SEC. 6. No child under fourteen years of age shall be so employed except during the vacations of the public schools, unless during the year next preceding such employment he shall have attended some public or private day school for at least twelve weeks, nor shall such employment continue unless such child shall, in each year, attend school as herein provided; and no child shall be so employed who does not present a certificate, made by, or under the direction of, said school committee, of his compliance with the requirements of this section.

Sec. 7. Every owner, superintendent or overseer of any establishment named in section 5 of this act, shall require and keep on file a certificate of the place and date of birth of every child under fifteen years of age employed therein, as nearly accurate as may be, so long as such child is so employed, which certificate shall also state, in the case of a child under fifteen years of age, the amount of his school attendance during the year next preceding such employment. The certificates herein mentioned shall be signed by a member of the school committee of the town where such attendance was had, or by some one authorized by such committee, and the form of said certificate shall be furnished by the secretary of the state board of education.

Sec. 8. Every owner, superintendent or overseer of any such establishment who employs or permits to be employed any child in violation of either of the two next preceding sections, and every parent or guardian who permits such employment, shall be fined not exceeding twenty dollars.

Sec. 9. The truant officers shall, at least once in every school term, and as often as the school committee require, visit the establishments described in section 5 of this act, in their respective towns, and ascertain whether the provisions of the four next preceding sections hereof are duly observed, and report all violations thereof to the school committee.

SEC. 10. The truant officers shall demand the names of the children under fifteen years of age employed in such establishments in their respective towns, and shall require the certificates of age and school attendance, prescribed in section 7 of this act, to be produced for their inspection; and a failure to produce such certificate shall be evidence that the employment of such child is illegal.

SEC. 11. Every owner, superintendent or overseer of any such establishment who employs, or permits to be employed therein, a child under fifteen years of age who cannot write his name, age and place of residence legibly, while the public schools in the town where such child lives are in session, shall for every such offence be fined not exceeding twenty dollars.

SEC. 12. The town councils of the several towns shall make all needful provisions and arrangements concerning habitual truants and children who may be found wandering about in the streets or public places therein, having no lawful occupation or business, not attending school and growing up in ignorance; and shall make such ordinances as will be most conducive to the welfare of such children and to the good order of such town; and shall designate or provide suitable places for the confinement, discipline and instruction of such children.

SEC. 13. Every minor convicted under an ordinance made under the provisions of section 12 of this act of being an habitual truant, or of wandering about in the streets and public places of a town, or of having no lawful employment or business, or of not attending school, and of growing up in ignorance, shall be committed to any institution of instruction or suitable place designated or provided for the purpose under the authority of said section 12, for a period not exceeding two years.

SEC. 14. Children so committed may, on satisfactory proof of amendment, or for other sufficient cause, be discharged from such institution or place by the court which committed them.

SEC. 15. The school committees of the several towns shall annually report to the state board of education whether their towns have made the provisions required by this act.

SEC. 16. All fines under the provisions of this act shall inure and be applied to the support of the public schools in the town where the offence was committed.

SEC. 17. The justice courts of the several towns shall have jurisdiction of all cases arising under this act.

SEC. 18. Chapter 60, and sections 21, 22, 23 and 24 of chapter 169 of the Public Statutes, and all other acts and parts of acts inconsistent herewith are hereby repealed; and this act shall take effect upon and after the first day of October, A. D. 1883.

www.ingramcontent.com/pod-product-compliance
Lightning Source LLC
Chambersburg PA
CBHW021119270326
41929CB00009B/950
* 9 7 8 3 7 4 4 6 6 6 9 7 8 *